FLORIDA DEVOTIONS

INSPIRATIONAL STORIES FROM THE SWAMP

DEL DUDUIT

IRON STREAM

Birmingham, Alabama

As a broadcaster of high school sports and a fan of college football, I can say this book by Del Duduit will connect with the everyday football fan. Del takes moments in the history of Florida football and applies biblical and Christian principles to each chapter. He takes great plays like the "Heave to Cleve" and tells us how to stay close to the Lord in our daily walk. And then he talks about how Tim Tebow won the Heisman Trophy and encourages the reader to set a great example as a follower of Christ. This book will not only appeal to the college football fan and the Florida football fan but to anyone who wants to be inspired.

—Mark Williams, sports manager, WNXT Radio

I'm a big fan of SEC football, so this devotional by Del Duduit is a perfect fit. Although I'm a Kentucky guy all the way, I appreciate the Florida Gators and how they play the game. I love this book and the way Del relives great moments in the history of the program. But what I love even more, is the way he puts an inspirational and motivational spin on it. Each devotion recaps a big game and then gives the reader something to think about and connects it to the moments. Then he challenges the reader with a call to action. You will be blessed with *Florida Devotions* whether you are a Gator fan, a football fan, or just a fan in general. The main thing in this book is that God is glorified and you are supplied with a playbook as a Christian to tackle each day.

—Robby Speer, cofounder and
executive director of Sports Reach

Let's get one thing straight: I am a Florida State man through and through. Chapter 21 in this book broke my heart because it brought back the memory of when Florida knocked off my beloved Seminoles 17–15. I still have nightmares because FSU was undefeated. That muffed punt was the turning point and led to the Florida win. But life goes on. And in this book, Del Duduit uses moments like these to encourage the Christian to be grateful and follow the Lord no matter what. I love football. I love the Florida and Florida State rivalry, and I love this devotional book.

—Mark "Coach" Prasek, host, PJNET.tv

This book is dedicated to my friend and Sunday school teacher Tom Smith. Your lessons are well prepared and delivered with love and compassion.

CONTENTS

ACKNOWLEDGMENTS

Several people played key roles in making this book a reality. I would like to thank the following for their efforts in bringing this book to you.

- ➤ My wife, Angie, for being the initial editor of this book and for her support.

- ➤ My agent, Cyle Young, for his work to get my work in front of the right people.

- ➤ My publisher, John Herring, for his trust and faith in me.

- ➤ My editors, Larry J. Leech II and Susan Cornell, for making this product better.

- ➤ The production crew at Iron Stream Media.

- ➤ My Lord and Savior for this exciting opportunity.

DAY 1
BEGIN YOUR JOURNEY

September 11, 1993: Florida 24, Kentucky 20

Therefore, if anyone is in Christ, he is a new creation.
The old has passed away; behold, the new has come.

—2 Corinthians 5:17

The Florida Gators couldn't give away the win on a Saturday night in Lexington, Kentucky. The Wildcat defense picked off seven Florida passes and still lost the game. While the Gators threw SEVEN interceptions, they somehow won the Southeastern Conference game, 24-20, at Commonwealth Stadium.

Gator quarterback Terry Dean threw four picks off and backup Danny Wuerffel threw three. But Wuerffel, who finished the game with 138 yards on a 10-of-22 performance, managed to find wide receiver Chris Doering on a 28-yard TD pass with three seconds left in the game to give the Gators the improbable win.

That game-winning pass was the reason Florida Head Coach Steve Spurrier gave the starting position to Wuerffel, a red-shirt freshman from Fort Walton Beach High School, who led his team against Tennessee the following week.

This started something special in Gainesville, Florida. When his career as a Gator ended, Wuerffel had set the bar high. He led his team to four SEC Championships and one

National Championship. He also won the prestigious Heisman Trophy, the Maxwell Award, the Johnny Unitas Golden Arm Award, and the Walter Camp Award and was named the *Sporting News* Player of the Year in 1996.

His chance to shine might never have happened if not for Dean's four interceptions. His chances improved drastically when he capitalized on his opportunity and gave it his all, throwing a miraculous touchdown pass with three seconds to play in the game, at a time when defeat seemed imminent.

> For I know the plans I have for you, declares the LORD, plans for welfare and not for evil, to give you a future and a hope. —Jeremiah 29:11

TWO BITS, FOUR BITS, SIX BITS, A DOLLAR

Where does your story begin? Have you been in a place where the odds were stacked against you to pull off the big win? Do you feel the need to have someone come off the bench and rescue your team—and you? Has life reached the point where all your passes are picked off by the enemy? Maybe you are facing health issues, or perhaps you lost your job, or an important relationship is facing a fourth down and 20 yards to go. You've tried many options, but your chances of victory keep slipping away.

THE GATOR CHOMP

As you look to your bench for reinforcements, you see One player who can bring you a championship, One player who can answer your prayers, One player who can bring you hope and joy. You've tried every available game plan, but you can't get any closer to the goal line. With three seconds left to play in the game, what will you do? The best decision you can make is to put Jesus Christ under center in your life and watch for game-changing miracles to happen.

1. You will have peace of mind: In today's uncertain world, the Lord offers a wonderful peace only His children can possess. This does not mean you will live a life free from trials and problems, but it guarantees you a unique joy and happiness as you go through life's journey.

2. You will experience victory and true forgiveness: When the Lord forgives you of your sins, you will feel an enormous weight lifted from your shoulders. Then you can offer mercy to those who have wronged you. There is no better feeling than victory and freedom from bitterness. "In him we have redemption through his blood, the forgiveness of our trespasses, according to the riches of his grace" (Ephesians 1:7).

3. You will find happiness and hope: Hope is wonderful. It's the reason you get up every day. Today might be that day. A new job. A new relationship. A new opportunity to make a difference. A reason to smile and have a positive impact on someone. When you have hope, you have it all. "May the God of hope fill you with all joy and peace in believing, so that by the power of the Holy Spirit you may abound in hope" (Romans 15:13).

4. You will have a personal relationship beyond measure: You can go to Jesus in prayer, and He will listen and offer advice through His Word, the Bible. There is no better friend or Father who can help us as much as He

can and will. There is something special about a personal relationship with someone you trust. The Lord died for you so you can be free.

5. You will have eternal life in heaven: This is the best benefit of serving Christ. When the game of life is over and you have tossed the game-winning TD with three seconds left, you can go into the winning locker room with a big smile and find eternal rest. This is real. The playbook is real. And eternity is real. "For God so loved the world, that he gave his only Son, that whoever believes in him should not perish but have eternal life" (John 3:16).

You can come off the bench and earn your starting position by letting the coach know you want to play. Whisper a prayer and ask God to lead your team. And when the game is over, you will have a robe and crown that is more valuable than all the awards, trophies, and championships that Wuerffel earned.

DAY 2

STOP AND POP—THE DEVIL

January 2, 1997: Florida 52, FSU 20
National Championship Game

And do not lead us into temptation, but deliver us from the evil one. For Yours is the kingdom and the power and the glory forever. Amen. —Matthew 6:13 NKJV

The 1997 Sugar Bowl was a blowout. Florida cruised to a 52-20 win to claim the National Championship over its rival the Seminoles at the Louisiana Superdome in New Orleans.

But a few weeks earlier, the two battled it out at Doak Campbell Stadium in Tallahassee, Florida, where No. 2-ranked Florida State knocked off top-ranked Florida, 24-21.

A month later, on January 2, the Seminoles came into the game with a No. 1 ranking while the Gators were the third-best team in the nation.

In their previous contest, Florida quarterback Danny Wuerffel was sacked six times and often hit behind the line of scrimmage.

Gators Head Coach Steve Spurrier used the shotgun formation in the National Championship game, and it gave his team an advantage over the Seminoles. In 1997, the shotgun was not used as much as it is now.

During the second quarter, Florida wide receiver Ike Hilliard hauled in a pass from Wuerffel in what appeared to be a routine play. But Hilliard did something different. He noticed the two FSU defenders closing in on him. He caught the pass and then somehow stopped on a dime. The momentum of the two defenders caused them to crash into each other. Hilliard then dashed 31 yards into the end zone for the score and the 24-10 lead.

This moment was forever etched in stone as the "stop and pop" play. Hilliard stopped and the two defenders popped into each other.

Wuerffel was named the Sugar Bowl MVP and threw for 306 yards and three touchdowns—all to Hilliard, who posted seven catches for 150 yards.

In the postgame press conference, FSU Head Coach Bobby Bowden said one of the most memorable quotes in all of college football. "Now do you see why we didn't want to play them again?"

> But the Lord is faithful, who will establish you and guard you from the evil one. —2 Thessalonians 3:3 NKJV

TWO BITS, FOUR BITS, SIX BITS, A DOLLAR

Maybe you have gone through a recent defeat and now face a rematch. There are many challenges in your life that can cause you to lose a game:

➢ Have you ever lost your temper and it hurt your witness?

➢ Have you said something to or about someone that caused hurt?

➤ Do you have impure thoughts?

➤ Have you given into temptation in an area of your life that you thought was off-limits?

➤ Have you stopped reading your Bible?

➤ Have you stopped praying or going to church?

➤ Have you lost interest in serving the Lord?

The rematch is scheduled, and it's for the National Championship of your soul.

THE GATOR CHOMP

When life hits you with circumstances you didn't see coming, and you are surprised with a loss, pick yourself up off the turf, and make some adjustments to catch the enemy off guard the next time.

When you anticipate the devil coming at you from all sides, stop and pop and head to the end zone.

1. Always remember your identity in Christ. In Ephesians 6:13–14, Paul gave some wonderful advice: "Therefore take up the whole armor of God, that you may be able to withstand in the evil day, and having done all, to stand. Stand therefore, having girded your waist with truth, having put on the breastplate of righteousness" (NKJV). Stand firm in who you are as a believer in Christ. Whatever controls your heart controls your identity. As long as you keep the Lord in the center of your life, you have an identity that Satan cannot tackle. Stop and pop.

2. Read the Word of God a little more each day: This is your playbook. You can find razzle-dazzle and flea-flicker plays inside the Bible. Paul describes the Word of God as a sword. Your ability to overcome the devil's defenders is proportionate to your knowledge of God's Word. Trying to fend off the forces of evil without reading God's playbook is like running onto the gridiron without your helmet and pads. You will lose. Instead, be prepared. Stop and pop.

3. Pray often and consistently, even when you don't feel like it: This is your main weapon when battling against Satan. In the game of football, you need to possess the pigskin to win. In the game of life, you must view prayer as the key to victory. Paul tells you in Ephesians 6:18 to pray in the Spirit at all times. Pastor Samuel Chadwick wrote, "The one concern of the devil is to keep saints from prayer." A good prayer life is the ultimate stop and pop.

4. Witness to others about God's goodness: This will help and strengthen you on your journey. When you tell friends and coworkers what the Lord has done in your life, it will embolden you and give you the responsibility to live up to what you say. Stop and pop.

5. Praise your way to victory: When you are down on the scoreboard, give thanks to the Lord for His goodness. This will prepare you for the next battle. When you can give glory to God for all His benefits to you even in a loss, you will be better equipped for the next game. Coach Spurrier adjusted for the next game

with FSU and won. He took the lessons from the loss and used them to his advantage. You can do the same. Stop and pop.

God does not leave you alone in your battle against the devil. Christ is our resurrected Savior who has the power to defeat Satan and defend you against his unfair attacks. You have an identity through your relationship with Jesus that is established on a solid foundation. Remember your identity in Christ, read the Word of God, and pray to your heavenly Father. Stand up as a solid witness and always be ready to give Him praise, and you will be ready to stop and pop the devil to go into the end zone for the victory. And afterward, Satan and his forces will think twice about playing you again.

DAY 3
MAKE THE BIG IMPACT PLAY

January 8, 2009: Florida 24, Oklahoma 14
National Championship Game

Ye are the light of the world. A city that is set on an hill cannot be hid. —Matthew 5:14 KJV

It was the No. 1 Oklahoma Sooners against No. 2-ranked Florida Gators in the first-ever meeting between the two schools, who each came in with a Heisman Trophy winner. The 2009 FedEx BCS National Championship was on the line in front of more than 78,000 fans at Dolphin Stadium in Miami, Florida.

Florida's kicker Jonathan Phillips nailed a 27-yard field goal for a 17-14 lead with 10:45 to play in the game.

Now, Oklahoma's quarterback Sam Bradford, the 2008 Heisman Trophy winner, had to rally his team for a chance to take home the title. The Sooners drove down the field and before they knew it, the Gators had to make another goal-line stand.

Bradford fired at his target, wide receiver Juaquin Iglesias, for what was going to be a go-ahead touchdown. But Florida's Ahmad Black made the play of the game and stripped the ball away from Iglesias for the interception.

From there, it was vintage Tim Tebow. The gutsy 2007 Heisman Trophy winner led the Gators in an eleven-play drive that culminated with his trademark jump-pass touchdown to David Nelson from 4 yards out for a 24-14 lead.

Tebow, who was named the offensive MVP of the game, finished the contest with two touchdown passes, while Percy Harvin ran in one score from 2 yards to give the Gators their second BCS National Championship in three seasons.

But it was all made possible by Black's amazing play.

For God hath not given us the spirit of fear; but of power, and of love, and of a sound mind. —2 Timothy 1:7 KJV

TWO BITS, FOUR BITS, SIX BITS, A DOLLAR

Many people take pride in a job well done, but some desire to be in the limelight for their actions more than others. Recognition is nice, but sometimes silent heroes are the ones who lead their team to victory. Black knew his role and rose to the occasion when the opportunity presented itself. If he had not come through in the clutch, his team may not have won the title. He did his job regardless of the fanfare and the applause. And because he did what he did, his team had the chance to win. He didn't score, but he stopped the opposition from reaching the goal line. Are you happy to quietly do your job and influence others? Or do you want everyone to know about your accomplishments?

THE GATOR CHOMP

Black gave his team momentum. Inspiration. A chance. He gave them one more opportunity. He had a positive impact on his team. What about you? What influence do you have on those around you? Are you ready to rip the ball away from the enemy? Are you prepared to make the big play? Here are some tips to make sure you are ready on game day.

1. Help others: Put aside your own personal wants and focus on those who need help. When you take time to help a friend in need, you can look at yourself in the mirror and know you had the strength to put someone else first. "And now abideth faith, hope, charity, these three; but the greatest of these is charity" (1 Corinthians 13:13 KJV).

2. Treat others how you wish to be treated: The Golden Rule is not just an old saying; it always applies in everyday life. When you master the art of kindness to those who are not kind to you, then you might be ready to make the big play at the goal line. "The hand of the diligent shall bear rule: but the slothful shall be under tribute" (Proverbs 12:24 KJV).

3. Be thankful: Show gratitude for what you have and for what you do NOT have. God always knows best, and you may not understand now why He says no. But later He shows you that His plan was good. He blesses us with His hand of protection, and His plans are always better than ours. God gives you what you need.

4. Forgive: Unforgiveness is a self-imposed emotional prison. There's nothing more liberating than to break the chains of bitterness and offer mercy to someone who has wronged you, even if that person does not apologize. This is hard, but it's vital to keep the sweet peace in your heart. Without it, you will not make the big interception and put your team in a position for the win. "And be ye kind one to another, tenderhearted, forgiving one

another, even as God for Christ's sake hath forgiven you" (Ephesians 4:32 KJV).

5. Be active: In your church. In your community. In the lives of your family. When you understand that life is not about you, then you are on the right track to make a big impact on those around you. Instead of playing your weekly round of golf, skip once in a while and volunteer at a homeless shelter. Giving to others is more rewarding, and you won't need to take a mulligan.

These suggestions are not all-inclusive. But if you can master these top five items, you will be prepared to make the big play at the goal line and make a positive impact on your team.

DAY 4

JUMP FOR JOY

October 7, 2006: Florida 23, LSU 10

May the God of hope fill you with all joy and peace in believing, so that by the power of the Holy Spirit you may abound in hope. —Romans 15:13

With thirty seconds left in the first half, freshman quarterback Tim Tebow faced a second down and goal from the 1-yard line against Louisiana State University. Tebow took the snap from the shotgun and appeared to run the ball to the left side. But the 230-pound QB stopped, jumped in the air, double-clutched, and threw a pass to Tate Casey for the touchdown and the lead.

Sports broadcaster Kevin Harlan was on the mic for CBS and shouted, "Oh my gosh! That looks like 1955."

The "jump pass" caught everyone by surprise, and it was a sign of exciting things to come from the iconic player. He pulled it off again to perfection in the 2009 FedEx BCS National Championship Game at Dolphin Stadium in Miami, Florida.

This time, Tebow's jump pass found David Nelson in the end zone and sealed the deal for a 24-14 win over No. 2 Oklahoma and the National Championship.

The play always worked and made the Gators fans jump for joy every time he pulled it off.

A joyful heart is good medicine, but a crushed spirit dries up the bones. ——Proverbs 17:22

TWO BITS, FOUR BITS, SIX BITS, A DOLLAR

Do you feel the defenders coming at you to bring you down before you reach the end zone? Are there times in your life when you are faced with a fourth-down-and-goal? People face battles every day. You cannot hide from them, and they must be dealt with head on. You might think the defense is about to stop you. But there is one thing you can do to help you through the challenges: Jump. Jump for joy.

THE GATOR CHOMP

What does it mean to jump for joy? Does it literally mean to jump? Maybe. But you don't have to jump to give praise and honor to the Lord. Praising God doesn't remove your problems, but it will give you the encouragement and attitude to trust Christ to catch the touchdown pass when you jump in the air. How can you jump for joy? There are many ways. Here are some suggestions on how you can incorporate your own "jump pass" to secure a win over the enemy.

1. Be happy for others: When something good happens to someone in your circle, be happy for them and help celebrate their victory. Cheer them on when they accomplish goals, and especially encourage them when they give their hearts to the Lord. Put aside any envy or negative feelings and rejoice with them. Don't be jealous or covet their good news. Your time is coming. "Instead of your shame there shall be a double portion; instead of

dishonor they shall rejoice in their lot; therefore in their land they shall possess a double portion; they shall have everlasting joy. For I the LORD love justice; I hate robbery and wrong; I will faithfully give them their recompense, and I will make an everlasting covenant with them" (Isaiah 61:7–8).

2. Put a song in your heart: Singing a melody each day will lift your spirits and keep you going in the right direction. Choose music with a positive and hopeful message that will put you in a good place and keep you motivated. Satan wants to stuff you at the line of scrimmage. Fake him out and let him hear you sing praises unto the King of Kings.

3. Give of your time and serve others: Donating your time, your most valuable asset, makes a huge difference in your life and in the lives of those you impact. Combine this with a financial donation, and the blessings will multiply. When God is good to you, consider paying it forward and help others in need. "Give, and it will be given to you. Good measure, pressed down, shaken together, running over, will be put into your lap. For with the measure you use it will be measured back to you" (Luke 6:38).

4. Ask: When you pray, thank God for your past blessings and make your petitions known. Be specific but be open to His plan and His provision in His way and His time. Don't suggest how or when He should answer your prayers, but rather trust Him and wait on Him to do what is best for you in your situation. "In that day you will ask

nothing of me. Truly, truly, I say to you, whatever you ask of the Father in my name, he will give it to you. Until now you have asked nothing in my name. Ask, and you will receive, that your joy may be full" (John 16:23–24).

5. Praise: Fellowship with other believers in the house of God and praising your heavenly father can lift you out of the darkest valleys. Focus on God, be thankful for His blessings on your life, and take a break from your problems. Who knows? You might even jump for joy a time or two. "With my mouth I will give great thanks to the LORD; I will praise him in the midst of the throng" (Psalm 109:30).

Tim Tebow made the "jump pass" a thing of beauty. He used it as a weapon to catch the defense off guard. He always did it when the defense did not expect it to happen. When you jump for joy, you send a message to the devil that he can't stop you from reaching the end zone. When you jump for joy, you win every time.

DAY 5
OVERCOME THE ODDS

November 22, 1997: Florida 32, FSU 29

These things I have spoken unto you, that in me ye might have peace. In the world ye shall have tribulation: but be of good cheer; I have overcome the world.
—John 16:33 KJV

Florida State rolled into Ben Hill Griffin Stadium in Gainesville, Florida, as the clear favorite to win. The Seminoles were undefeated and ranked No. 2, and the only obstacle that stood in their way of winning a National Championship was the No. 10-ranked Gators (8-2).

FSU Coach Bobby Bowden's defense was one of the best in the nation. Experts in college football and oddsmakers in Las Vegas had predicted the game would be a blowout and the Seminoles would roll over the Gators and play for a national title.

The previous year, the Gators lost in the National Championship to Nebraska, 62-24, in the Tostitos Fiesta Bowl. But this season, Florida Head Coach Steve Spurrier knew his team would not play for a chance at the big show because they had already suffered losses to Georgia and LSU during the regular season. The Gators were playing for pride and honor, and they did not want their FSU rivals to have a chance at the national title.

The game atmosphere was tense, and the play was electric. Both teams battled back and forth.

When FSU kicker Sebastian Janikowski nailed a field goal with two minutes left in the game for a 4-point lead, the chances of escaping from The Swamp looked pretty good. Following the score, Janikowski looked up at the Florida fans and mocked them with his rendition of the Gator Chomp.

On the first play from scrimmage after the kickoff, Florida quarterback Doug Johnson went downfield with a pass and found Jacquez Green for a 63-yard completion. Moments later, running back Fred Taylor scored his fourth touchdown of the game and pushed Florida to a 32-29 lead.

Florida State had little time for a drive to put themselves in a position to tie the game. But Thad Busby had other plans and picked off a pass to secure the win for the Gators.

Spurrier's team was prepared and overcame the odds to win one of the most exciting games in history.

> Wherefore seeing we also are compassed about with so great a cloud of witnesses, let us lay aside every weight, and the sin which doth so easily beset us, and let us run with patience the race that is set before us.
>
> —Hebrews 12:1 KJV

TWO BITS, FOUR BITS, SIX BITS, A DOLLAR

Throughout life, not everyone will cheer you on to success, and some may even wish for your demise. The devil takes pride and joy in trying to defeat God's children. He may use other people to say things to discourage you, and he will whisper in your ear at night that you don't matter, your situation is hopeless, and God has forgotten about you. The challenges may seem too hard to overcome, but you've got to huddle up and listen to the Lord's play calls.

THE GATOR CHOMP

The forces of evil use many different defensive formations and blitzes, such as money, gossip, lies, and temptations at will, to tackle you behind the line of scrimmage. When you are a believer, Satan will mock you and make you question the support of friends and family. He wants to drive a wedge between you and any hope you might have of achieving victory by using some of the following tactics:

1. Fear: It takes a lot of faith for you to take your hands off the ball and let the Lord throw the pass. But you can always trust Him to make the perfect play. "The LORD is my light and my salvation; whom shall I fear? The LORD is the strength of my life; of whom shall I be afraid?" (Psalm 27:1 KJV).

2. Anxiety: Important decisions and everyday stresses of life can lead to feelings of anxiety, leading you to become restless, tense, and exhausted. You know the Bible tells you not to worry, but you are also human. Always remember there is a higher power to lean on during these times. "Be careful for nothing; but in every thing by prayer and supplication with thanksgiving let your requests be made known unto God" (Philippians 4:6 KJV).

3. Depression: This condition is real. Some spiritual leaders may tell you this happens because you are not

walking close enough to the Lord. But be aware that this condition can come crashing down on you after tragedies occur or even result from chemical imbalances that require a doctor's care. While you should always look to God to help bring you through these valleys, don't be ashamed to seek the help of your family physician and a trusted Christian counselor. Seek out friends who will honor your privacy, hold you up in support and encouragement, and refrain from spreading gossip about you. "Fear thou not; for I am with thee: be not dismayed; for I am thy God: I will strengthen thee; yea, I will help thee; yea, I will uphold thee with the right hand of my righteousness" (Isaiah 41:10 KJV).

4. The past: This one can haunt you forever unless you sling it downfield for 63 yards and let the Master catch it to put you in solid field position. Others might try to remind you of your past mistakes, but the Lord will always forgive and forget if you ask. "If we confess our sins, he is faithful and just to forgive us our sins, and to cleanse us from all unrighteousness" (1 John 1:9 KJV).

5. Sin: When you know the right thing to do, and you choose not to do it, you are disobeying God. But when you seek forgiveness, change your way of life, and alter your sinful habits, ask Christ to lead you. He will give you joy and peace of mind. Remember that He loves you so much that He made the ultimate sacrifice, and He gives you multiple chances to choose Him as the Lord of your life. Don't take a time-out. Serve Him faithfully. "For God so loved the world, that he gave his only

begotten Son, that whosoever believeth in him should not perish, but have everlasting life" (John 3:16 KJV).

Florida was not supposed to win the game against FSU. The Seminoles were supposed to give the Gators a thrashing and head to the National Championship. But that did not happen. And for those who don't give you much of a chance, remind them that Jesus Christ gives the best Gator Chomp around.

DAY 6
BLOCK OUT THE ENEMY

November 11, 2006: Florida 17, South Carolina 16

Do not give the devil a foothold. ——Ephesians 4:27 NIV

What a moment. Florida defensive end Jarvis Moss jumped as high as he could and reached his arms for the heavens. His prayer was answered when he blocked a potential game-winning 48-yard field goal attempt by South Carolina kicker Ryan Succop.

The 6'7" Moss from Denton, Texas, secured the 17-16 win over the Gamecocks in front of more than 90,000 fans at Ben Hill Griffin Stadium in Gainesville, Florida.

This heroic act was the second of two blocks he made in the game—and the third overall in the contest for the Gators. Earlier in the fourth quarter, Moss batted down an extra-point attempt from Succop that left South Carolina with a 16-10 lead after Mike Davis scored his second TD of the game.

Following the score, Florida freshman quarterback Tim Tebow went to work. On a fourth down and one near midfield, Tebow plowed ahead for the first down to keep the drive alive.

Chris Leak put together a 17-yard burst and an 8-yard run to extend the drive. Then Tebow rumbled for a 12-yard TD. The extra point was good, and Florida led, 17-16.

In the first half of the game, Gator defensive tackle Ray McDonald blocked a 47-yard field goal attempt by Succop.

The three blocks stopped the Gamecocks from potentially scoring seven points.

The win by Florida ruined the return of former Head Coach Steve Spurrier to The Swamp and helped give second-year coach Urban Meyer the boost he needed to guide his team to a National Championship.

Submit yourselves, then, to God. Resist the devil, and he will flee from you. —James 4:7 NIV

TWO BITS, FOUR BITS, SIX BITS, A DOLLAR

Maybe you have enjoyed a close walk with the Lord over the years. You love to use the talents God gave you to glorify the King of Kings, and it puts a smile on your face. All may appear to be right in your world. Your job is going well, and your family is healthy. But out of nowhere, the devil lines up to kick a gimme chip shot. This would really catch you by surprise, and the loss would mean the end of your championship-season run. Will you make the block?

THE GATOR CHOMP

Christians are not strong enough by themselves to make the big play. Here are some tips to reach your arms for the heavens and knock the ball down to the ground.

1. Show confidence: You have the best defender in the world on your team! God is your best player, coach, and supporter. The devil will lie and tell you that you don't deserve God's blessings, but remember that when your sins are forgiven, you instantly make the trade from the

worst team in the league to the best. Christ throws your sins into the sea of forgetfulness, so don't go fishing for them. "Dear friends, if our hearts do not condemn us, we have confidence before God and receive from him anything we ask, because we keep his commands and do what pleases him" (1 John 3:21–22 NIV).

2. Prepare and expect: This comes by reading the Word of God, praying, and attending church on a regular basis. God is the creator and master of the universe, and nothing is too small for Him to tackle. No kick is too high for Him to block. Keep your defensive strategy simple . . . ask Him! "You desire but do not have, so you kill. You covet but you cannot get what you want, so you quarrel and fight. You do not have because you do not ask God" (James 4:2 NIV).

3. Realize you are no match for the devil: Never allow pride to get in your way. You alone cannot block the kick. You need the Lord to bust through the line and clear the path for you to jump. When a player admits he is weak, then he indeed becomes stronger. When you work as a team, great things can be accomplished. Ask Jesus for strength and ask a friend to join you in prayer and seek His will together.

4. Praise your way through your trials: You cannot block the kick if your arms are dropped to your side. Get to church and join in fellowship with your church family. Lift your arms in praise to the Father and ask Him to help you block the devil's kicks. "Because your love is better than life, my lips will glorify you. I will praise

you as long as I live, and in your name I will lift up my hands" (Psalm 63:3–4 NIV).

5. Remember that the Lord wins in the end: When you get discouraged about unexpected circumstances that leave you in a position to lose, take a moment and look at the box score in the book of Revelation. GOD WINS!

When Moss blocked the kick on that last play, he preserved the win. But remember that it took a team effort to put 17 points on the board leading up to that moment. His earlier block combined with McDonald's play kept the Gamecocks off the board. When the devil comes at you, raise your arms toward the sky and knock down the kick.

DAY 7

CRUSH THE LIES OF THE DEVIL

January 1, 1994: Florida 41, West Virginia 7

You are of your father the devil, and your will is to do your father's desires. He was a murderer from the beginning, and does not stand in the truth, because there is no truth in him. When he lies, he speaks out of his own character, for he is a liar and the father of lies.

—John 8:44

The eighth-ranked Florida Gators rolled into the Superdome in New Orleans, Louisiana, and rolled over No. 2-ranked West Virginia, 41-7, to claim the Sugar Bowl crown.

At the time, the Gators' point total and margin of victory stats were the second largest in the history of the Sugar Bowl.

Florida running back Errict Rhett ran for 105 yards and scored three touchdowns, and was named the game's MVP. Quarterback Terry Dean threw for 255 yards and completed 22 of 37 attempts with one TD.

The Gators outplayed West Virginia in all facets of the game. But one particular moment stands out for most Florida fans when this game is mentioned.

The play they most vividly recall happened when WVU quarterback Darren Studstill scrambled to his left in the second quarter and tried to run upfield.

Florida linebacker Monty Grow had a full head of steam, coming in to smash Studstill with such force that the QB had to take his helmet over to the sideline because the chin strap was knocked up into a vertical position.

What a hit!

A lie from the devil can have a devastating impact if his hit catches you off guard, and it may force you to hold your head and look at your helmet to see if it's been damaged. Be careful not to believe the enemy's falsehoods.

> Be sober-minded; be watchful. Your adversary the devil prowls around like a roaring lion, seeking someone to devour. —1 Peter 5:8

TWO BITS, FOUR BITS, SIX BITS, A DOLLAR

The devil does not play fair. He will do all he can to bring misery and anguish into your life and keep you from having a close relationship with the Lord. The best play he has is to whisper lies to you, and he does the most when you are vulnerable or weak. He jumps on the opportunity to kick you when you're down, taking advantage of situations such as a job loss, health issues, or personal issues that he probably helped create. Lies. They can be hurtful and cause division.

THE GATOR CHOMP

When Satan tries to scramble around the truth and hand you a big fat lie, let the Lord come through the line and hit him so hard his helmet comes off and rolls around on the turf. Here are some of the enemy's popular topics:

1. Life is too busy for spiritual things: The devil will tell you that God understands that your life is chaotic, and it's OK if you don't have time to pray, read your Bible, or go to church. You've earned a break, and everyone deserves to kick back and relax a little. LIE! How would you feel if your spouse, children, or family went a day without speaking to you? Would you feel that something is off? Of course you would. It's not too difficult to set aside a few moments before the day begins to talk to the Master. In fact, He urges us to do this in His word. "Praying at all times in the Spirit, with all prayer and supplication. To that end, keep alert with all perseverance, making supplication for all the saints" (Ephesians 6:18).

2. You are unforgivable: The devil is good at sneaking into the huddle and telling you that you are not good enough. LIE! No matter what you have done in the past, if you ask the Lord to forgive you of your sins and allow Him to change you, then He will forgive. Never compare what you have done with the sins of others. Your story is unique. Your forgiveness is unique. Christ died for you. "I acknowledged my sin to you, and I did not cover my iniquity; I said, 'I will confess my transgressions to the LORD,' and you forgave the iniquity of my sin. Selah" (Psalm 32:5).

3. You are worthless: The devil wants you to lose hope, and he will tell you that even if God forgives you, no one else will give you a chance. They will expect you to fail, and they will not support you. LIE! How much does Christ love you? "For God so loved the world, that he gave his only Son, that whoever believes in him should not perish but have eternal life" (John 3:16).

4. You have plenty of time to get right with God: You can party hard and do all the bad stuff you want because you can always ask God to forgive you when you are old and on your deathbed. LIE! While you CAN accept Christ into your heart up until your last breath of life, why wait and take the chance? Life is short and precious, and you never know when your appointed time will come to die. Your choices have eternal consequences. Don't give the devil a second of your time. "For what will it profit a man if he gains the whole world and forfeits his soul? Or what shall a man give in return for his soul?" (Matthew 16:26).

5. God loves you too much to send you to hell: A loving God would not send anyone to a place of torment. You are good enough just as you are to skip into heaven. LIE! The ONLY way to eternal life is to accept Christ as your personal savior. God loves every soul He has created, but He has also given everyone free will to make their own decisions. Hell is a real place, and you must make the choice to live for God or play for the enemy. "And these will go away into eternal punishment, but the righteous into eternal life" (Matthew 25:46).

When you are a believer, the devil will try to get inside your head by repeating his many lies. His plan is to strike fast and often so you hear them so often that you start to believe them. When he comes to you in your time of weakness, remember that he is the father of all lies. God is the way, the truth, and the life. No one comes to the Father any other way than through the shed blood of Jesus Christ.

DAY 8
ADMIT WHEN YOU ARE WRONG

November 21, 1998: Florida State 23, Florida 12

Take heed to yourselves: If thy brother trespass against thee, rebuke him; and if he repent, forgive him. And if he trespass against thee seven times in a day, and seven times in a day turn again to thee saying, I repent; thou shalt forgive him. —Luke 17:3–4 KJV

During a heated rivalry game, it's not uncommon to see a scuffle or two break out, but when yellow flags come out a half hour before kickoff, you know the intensity is real.

Such was the case on this day at Doak Campbell Stadium in Tallahassee, Florida, when the fourth-ranked Gators came into town to square off against the No. 5-ranked Seminoles.

During pregame warm-up, both teams migrated to midfield on the Seminoles' logo. Within minutes, players started to shove each other. Punches began to fly, and the rumble ensued.

Two walk-on FSU players who were not even suited up in uniform got under the skin of Florida starting safety Tony George. All three players were ejected from the game before it even started.

George said he was upset because an assistant coach from FSU shoved him, and nothing was done. He later apologized for taking a swing at the assistant coach. Others reports stated Florida quarterback Doug Johnson heaved a football at FSU

Head Coach Bobby Bowden. Johnson said he was not throwing it at the coach, but he did apologize.

The Seminoles' defense proved to be the factor in the actual contest and went on to keep the Gators to 12 points, while the offense put up 23 en route to the win.

"To walk out on the field and think you're going to play and then have this game taken away from you, it really hurts," George said to a sportswriter. "You wish you could have it back, but you can't."[1]

He did, however, admit he was wrong. So did Johnson.

Have you ever had to apologize? Is there something you need to get off your conscience?

Follow peace with all men, and holiness, without which no man shall see the Lord: Looking diligently lest any man fail of the grace of God; lest any root of bitterness springing up trouble you, and thereby many be defiled. —Hebrews 12:14–15 KJV

TWO BITS, FOUR BITS, SIX BITS, A DOLLAR

Have you ever hurt someone? Chances are you have. Most likely, you have been hurt, too, but when you wrong someone, you need to step up and make it right. A sincere apology is not a sign of weakness but rather an indication of strength and character. Take responsibility for your actions and be considerate of what you do and say to others.

---

[1] Michael Mayo, "Hits Start with Pregame Brawl," *South Florida Sun Sentinel*, November 21, 1998, https://www.sun-sentinel.com/news/fl-xpm-1998-11-22-9811220029-story.html

THE GATOR CHOMP

Have you ever said anything about someone behind his back and he found out about it? Author Dale Carnegie wrote, "When we are wrong—and that will be surprisingly often, if we are honest with ourselves—let's admit our mistakes quickly and with enthusiasm." Enthusiasm? Really? He is saying to be courageous and eager to make it right. Here are some ways to be sincere when you say, "I'm sorry."

1. Acknowledge the pain: The hardest part of an apology might be to admit you hurt someone. Never minimize the sensitivities of others or blame them for your mistakes. Take responsibility when you hurt someone with your actions or words and know that the damage you inflict is real. "Rejoice with them that do rejoice, and weep with them that weep" (Romans 12:15 KJV).

2. Be specific about what you are apologizing about: Stay away from words like *if* and *maybe*. These can trigger an unintended reaction. Own up to your poor decision, and don't downplay your actions or make excuses.

3. Accept the consequences: Humility plays the biggest role in this step. This is not a negotiation. When you confess your wrongdoings, you must accept the ramifications of your actions. Stand up as an adult and accept the consequences whether you deem them fair or unjust. Be patient and give the other person space to share their feelings. When they see you are sincere, doors might swing open to begin to mend your relationship.

4. Make it right: If restoration involves a financial obligation, pay your dues. If you don't know the actual cost,
   then guess. "If a man shall steal an ox, or a sheep, and kill
   it, or sell it; he shall restore five oxen for an ox, and four
   sheep for a sheep" (Exodus 22:1 KJV).

5. Learn your lesson: An apology means nothing if you
   keep repeating the same action. Back up your words
   with true change that will earn their trust. Show them
   they can count on you to do better.

When you sincerely apologize, you recognize your mistakes and
work to make things better. Life is a journey. It's full of incomplete passes and safety blitzes. But remember, your journey as a
believer started when you asked Christ to forgive your sins and
live in your heart. Salvation does not make you perfect——but
it does make you forgiven. Show courage by admitting when
you are wrong. Embrace the gospel and gain true freedom by
showing humility, sacrifice, and gratitude for forgiveness.

DAY 9
THE PROMISE

September 27, 2008: Ole Miss 31, Florida 30

For all the promises of God find their Yes in him. That is why it is through him that we utter our Amen to God for his glory. ——2 Corinthians 1:20

The 2008 season was not supposed to go like this——or was it?

The No. 4-ranked undefeated Gators hosted unranked Ole Miss in the fourth game on the regular schedule. The 90,000-plus fans at Ben Hill Griffin Stadium thought this game was another stepping-stone to a perfect season. After all, Florida was a 22-point favorite going into the game.

They thought wrong.

Ole Miss stunned the crowd and the college football world with a 31-30 upset. The Gators fell to No. 12 in the rankings.

But that was not the end of the story.

After the game, Tim Tebow, Florida's quarterback and leader, spoke from the heart at the press conference.[2]

I just want to say one thing to the fans and everybody in Gator Nation. I'm sorry. Extremely sorry. We were hoping for an undefeated season. That was my goal. It's something

---

[2] John Duffley, "'The Promise' Speech Cemented Tim Tebow's Legacy," Fanbuzz.com, September 27, 2021, https://fanbuzz.com/college-foot-ball/sec/florida/on-this-day-tebows-promise/.

Florida's never done here. But I promise you one thing: a lot of good will come out of this.

You have never seen any player in the entire country play as hard as I will play the rest of the season, and you'll never see someone push the rest of the team as hard as I will push everybody the rest of the season. You'll never see a team play harder than we will the rest of the season. God bless.

This was his promise. This was his commitment to himself, the team, and the fans.

And he backed it up.

The Gators ran the table the rest of the season, knocking off No. 3 LSU by 30 points and No. 8 Georgia by 39 points. They defeated South Carolina by 50, Florida State by 30, and No. 1 Alabama, 31-20, to win the conference title and move to the ultimate college football game.

They capped the season by winning the BCS National Championship game over No. 2 Oklahoma, 24-14, and Tebow was named the Offensive Player of the Game.

Promises made. Promises kept.

The Lord has also made some big promises to you—and He always backs them up.

When you pass through the waters, I will be with you; and through the rivers, they shall not overwhelm you; when you walk through fire you shall not be burned, and the flame shall not consume you. —Isaiah 43:2

TWO BITS, FOUR BITS, SIX BITS, A DOLLAR

Maybe you expected a perfect life, much like the Gator fans had expected a perfect season. But somewhere along the way, you were handed an unexpected defeat. There are many scenarios that could come into play: the loss of a loved one, a health issue, or another tragedy. No one is perfect and no one lives a perfect life, no matter what you see on social media.

THE GATOR CHOMP

When life hands you a horrible defeat, how will you respond? Will you take the easy way out and give up? This is the scenario the devil is rooting for, and he never expects you to rise to the occasion. Or will you face the music and promise to do better? If the situation is your fault, will you own it and take responsibility? When you start to doubt your salvation, always turn to the Word of God to remind you of His promises to give you assurance and hope. Here are just a few to remind you that the Lord has everything under control.

1. God will be with you through every trial: Even when you feel alone or lost, the Lord is there. "Have I not commanded you? Be strong and courageous. Do not be frightened, and do not be dismayed, for the LORD your God is with you wherever you go" (Joshua 1:9).

2. God has a good plan for you: Tebow said in the press conference that something good would come out of the loss. The same holds true for you. Even if you mess up or are defeated, God has something good in store for you to learn from your experience. "For I know the plans I have

for you, declares the LORD, plans for welfare and not for evil, to give you a future and a hope" (Jeremiah 29:11).

3. God provides you with weapons to fight spiritual warfare: But remember, it's up to you to use them. You have to want to win. You must have a desire to capture the trophy. "For God gave us a spirit not of fear but of power and love and self-control" (2 Timothy 1:7).

4. God is loving and kind to His children: He provides shelter during the storm. He is a refuge and a place of comfort. "'For the mountains may depart and the hills be removed, but my steadfast love shall not depart from you, and my covenant of peace shall not be removed,' says the LORD, who has compassion on you" (Isaiah 54:10).

5. God is faithful and just: The Lord does not promise a life of treasures and success. But He does promise to be with you through the good and the bad. "Let us hold fast the confession of our hope without wavering, for he who promised is faithful" (Hebrews 10:23).

God always keeps His promises, even when you break your promises to Him. He never gives up on you, and He always expects you to determine in your heart to give Him your best effort, especially after a loss. He will never leave you nor forsake you. You can always count on Him.

DAY 10
WHAT WE REALLY DESERVE

January 8, 2007: Florida 41, Ohio State 14
Tostitos BCS National Championship Game

Who Himself bore our sins in His own body on the
tree, that we, having died to our sins, might live for
righteousness—by whose stripes you were healed.

—1 Peter 2:24 NKJV

Top-ranked Ohio State was supposed to roll over the Gators
in the BCS National Championship Game at the University of
Phoenix Stadium in Scottsdale, Arizona.

According to many experts, Florida did not even deserve
to play in the big game. After all, Florida went into the final
week ranked fourth, while Ohio State (No. 1), USC (No. 2),
and Michigan (No. 3) rounded out the top four.

The Trojans of USC lost to UCLA, 13-9, while the Gators
defeated No. 9 Arkansas, 38-28, and the Wolverines were idle.

When the final polls came out, Florida jumped two spots
to No. 2, pitting them against the top team in the nation—the
Buckeyes.

Only .0101 points separated Florida and Michigan.
However, the Wolverines had lost the Big Ten Championship to
OSU, and many experts believed a team that could not win its
conference should not compete for a national crown.

Was Florida good enough to match up with Ohio State? Should they even be playing the Buckeyes?

These questions fueled Florida Coach Urban Meyer's desire to win, and all the pregame talk served to motivate Gator Nation all the more.

When the game ended, there was no question about which team was the best.

Florida had stuffed Ohio State and won, 41-14.

The Gator defense chomped down on Ohio State's Heisman Trophy winner, quarterback Troy Smith and limited him to only 35 passing yards.

The Buckeye's high-powered offense was limited to just nineteen minutes time of possession and 82 total yards.

Florida proved they not only deserved to be in the game, but they showed everyone that they were the best team in the nation that day.

Just like the naysayers, others may think we are so awful that we don't deserve to be in the game. But God's grace and goodness through His gift of salvation make it possible for us to be victorious and live a hope-filled life. God always has the final say.

Looking unto Jesus, the author and finisher of our faith, who for the joy that was set before Him endured the cross, despising the shame, and has sat down at the right hand of the throne of God. —Hebrews 12:2 NKJV

TWO BITS, FOUR BITS, SIX BITS, A DOLLAR

What do you expect from your heavenly Father? Do you believe He owes you a good life? A good job? A good family? A big home or a new boat? Or are you humble and appreciative of His goodness? It's easy to grow complacent and have an attitude of entitlement after God has blessed you so much already. But don't lose sight of the fact that everything you have is because God has allowed you to have it.

THE GATOR CHOMP

Nobody deserves the divine provision of God. "Every good gift and every perfect gift is from above, and comes down from the Father of lights" (James 1:17 NKJV).

Do you show God how much you appreciate what He has done for you, or do you take the blessings of the Lord for granted? Stick to His game plan for your life, and practice the following fundamentals to increase your chances for a victory:

1. Attend church regularly: You can't win a football game unless you show up at the stadium. The same goes for your Christian walk. Teamwork and relationships help you stay strong when you attend church regularly. Strive for fellowship and harmony with your brothers and sisters in Christ to finish well.

2. Read His Word: You cannot be a successful player without studying the playbook. The same applies to your journey as a believer. Dive into the gospel each day and set aside time to study and focus on what God has for you. God has something new for you each day. "Let the word of Christ dwell in you richly in all wisdom, teaching and admonishing one another in psalms and hymns and spiritual songs, singing with grace in your hearts to the Lord" (Colossians 3:16 NKJV).

3. Pray to Him daily: If you want to have a close relationship with the Father, you must talk to Him frequently. "Be anxious for nothing, but in everything by prayer and supplication, with thanksgiving, let your requests be made known to God; and the peace of God, which surpasses all understanding, will guard your hearts and minds through Christ Jesus" (Philippians 4:6–7 NKJV).

4. Worship Him faithfully: Praise is a great source of strength for a child of the King. You can lift your voice and hands to Him in praise in both the good times and the bad. Your problems may not disappear, but God will give you the courage to face them head on. When you give thanks and honor to the Lord no matter what's going on in your life, He will bless you. "I will praise You, O LORD, with my whole heart; I will tell of all Your marvelous works" (Psalm 9:1 NKJV).

5. Tell others about Him: Fans love to spread the good news when their team wins. You should also want to tell your friends, family, and coworkers the good news of the gospel. Ask God to give you the courage and wisdom you need to be a light to them and shine bright for the Lord.

If someone ever told you that you don't deserve God's blessings, they were right. No one deserves the goodness of the Lord. But His grace is free to all who ask. God sent His son to die on the cross for you and me. Three days later, He rose from the dead and offered us life everlasting. Does anyone deserve this precious gift? No. But God has shown mercy by providing it to all who call on his name.

DAY 11
LET THE LORD AVENGE YOUR LOSS

November 1, 2008: Florida 49, Georgia 10

Beloved, never avenge yourselves, but leave it to the wrath of God, for it is written, "Vengeance is mine, I will repay, says the Lord." —Romans 12:19

The No. 5-ranked Florida Gators needed to prove something to the No. 8 visiting Bulldogs of Georgia. The previous season, Georgia not only beat the Gators, 42-30, but they added insult to defeat.

When Bulldogs running back Knowshon Moreno scored a touchdown in the first quarter, it sparked a team-wide "celebration" dance in the end zone that was referred to as the "Gator Stomp."

Many viewed it as unsportsmanlike, and the Florida fans were outraged. Gators Head Coach Urban Meyer took note and figured one day there would be a payback.

On November 1, it was payback day.

Florida ran all over Georgia and had a commanding 14-3 lead at the break.

But in the third quarter, the Gators chomped down on the Bulldogs. Florida defensive back Joe Haden picked off Georgia QB Matthew Stafford and returned the ball to the 1-yard line.

Gator signal caller Tim Tebow plowed into the end zone to boost the lead to 21-3. Tebow then connected with receiver

Louis Murphy on a 44-yard touchdown pass for the 28-3 advantage in the third quarter.

As memories of the "Gator Stomp" performance from the previous season most likely danced inside his head, Meyer still wanted more. Tebow scored his third rushing touchdown of the game while his counterpart Stafford threw back-to-back interceptions. Following an Ahmad Black pick, Tebow found Percy Harvin on a 25-yard touchdown pass to keep the rout alive.

With the game clock winding down to end the game, Meyer used up all three of his time-outs to prolong the victory and send a loud message to Georgia's Head Coach Mark Richt and his Bulldogs to soak in the loss.

Meyer's revenge must have felt rewarding to Gator Nation. Have you ever wanted to get even?

Repay no one evil for evil, but give thought to do what is honorable in the sight of all. If possible, so far as it depends on you, live peaceably with all. Beloved, never avenge yourselves, but leave it to the wrath of God, for it is written, "Vengeance is mine, I will repay, says the Lord." To the contrary, "if your enemy is hungry, feed him; if he is thirsty, give him something to drink; for by so doing you will heap burning coals on his head." Do not be overcome by evil, but overcome evil with good.

—Romans 12:17–21

TWO BITS, FOUR BITS, SIX BITS, A DOLLAR

To seek revenge, or to try to get even, is a natural instinct. It's human nature to feel that way, especially when something bad happens to you and others delight in your misery. Perhaps someone told a lie about you, which led to significant consequences. Or a person took credit for something you did and received a reward for it. Sometimes life isn't fair, and it makes you want to scream loud and get even.

THE GATOR CHOMP

Obeying Christ isn't always easy. It can sometimes be extremely difficult. As a believer, you are instructed throughout the Bible to "turn the other cheek." This goes against every human instinct. While someone may well deserve a punch in the mouth, God says you must be nice. On top of that, you must love the person. Here are some ways to love the "unlovable" and avoid a total defeat from the devil.

1. Love others even when they don't deserve it: Two of the biggest commandments the Lord gives you are to love God and others. Instead of lashing out at the person who has done you wrong, use self-restraint and try to find common ground. When you are able to show love and mercy, you win. "The second is this: 'You shall love your neighbor as yourself.' There is no other commandment greater than these" (Mark 12:31).

2. Demonstrate grace: Isn't loving people enough when they have done you wrong? Remember that no person is perfect, and everyone makes mistakes. Maybe you made a bad decision or said some words that caused emotional harm to a friend or family member. You can use your past behavior to learn how to forgive others. To show grace means you understand that everyone can throw an interception. Show hope and compassion toward the ones who "celebrated" your defeat.

3. Pray for those who have delighted in your sorrows: Take these people to the Lord in prayer and ask Him to give you what you need to show them mercy. Ask God for strength and guidance, and the Lord will hear your cry and will send down comfort and peace. "But I say to you, Love your enemies and pray for those who persecute you" (Matthew 5:44).

4. Read the Word of God: The Lord was clear in the fifth chapter of Matthew about how to treat someone who you want to take revenge on. "But I say to you that everyone who is angry with his brother will be liable to judgment; whoever insults his brother will be liable to the council; and whoever says, 'You fool!' will be liable to the hell of fire" (Matthew 5:22). Ask yourself, "Is it worth the risk?"

5. Walk away: Be the bigger person and just don't say a word or engage in insults. This can be difficult to do when the carnal side of you wants to utter words or shove back. When a calm conversation cannot take place, just walk away or hang up the phone. Sometimes, when you say nothing at all, you convey a powerful message.

There are times when you must defend yourself, and God knows the difference. This does not mean to let anyone say anything about you or your family. It simply means that you value your walk with Christ over a confrontation that could have a negative impact on your witness. Turning the other cheek is not a sign of weakness but a sign of obedience.

DAY 12
DON'T SLAM ANYONE

November 26, 2011: Florida State 21, Florida 7

A man of quick temper acts foolishly, and a man of evil devices is hated. —Proverbs 14:17

Florida State University poured it on the Gators at Ben Hill Griffin Stadium, 21-7. The Seminoles scored two touchdowns on two Florida turnovers. And the Gators managed only 95 yards of total offense.

Florida quarterback John Brantley had a tough but short day on the field. He completed 9 of 15 passes for 104 yards, but he was picked off three times in the first half.

On one play, he was sandwiched between two Seminole defenders as he released a pass. He went to the ground and laid there. He slowly got up and was helped to the sidelines with a concussion and did not return to the game.

The Gators were frustrated as the game went on, and in the fourth quarter, the tension came to a boil.

Jermaine Thomas caught a short pass for the Seminoles and was headed upfield when Florida defender Matt Elam came in to make the tackle. He wrapped up Thomas and then body-slammed him to the turf out of bounds. The referees tossed yellow flags and penalized Florida 15 yards for roughness.

As a high school recruit, Elam committed to Florida, then to Florida State, then back again to the Gators. So when

Florida State's Greg Reid rushed up to him and got in his face, words were exchanged. Both players had to be restrained by teammates, and a brawl almost broke out.

The combination of losing their quarterback early in the game and falling behind on the board to the rivals on their home field took an emotional toll on the Gators and on Elam.

Have you ever lost your temper because you were losing badly to the enemy?

A soft answer turns away wrath, but a harsh word stirs up anger. —Proverbs 15:1

TWO BITS, FOUR BITS, SIX BITS, A DOLLAR

If you listen to the devil long enough, he will try to convince you that your situation is hopeless and there is no way out. Because he says you are a failure doesn't mean you are. He is the king of all liars, and he'll do anything to bring you down and make you feel sorry for yourself. You might find yourself in a similar situation. A day when nothing has gone right. Maybe you had an argument with a friend and had something go wrong at work that was your fault. Perhaps you lost the big deal you were trying to close or were cut off on your drive to work. All these circumstances arouse anger and frustration. In the flesh, you want to scream, shout, or even strike out at an object—or possibly at a person who has wronged you or received a promotion you thought you deserved. Or maybe some minor issue has been stuck in your craw for weeks. In any case, you want to body-slam the opponent and get rid of your frustrations.

THE GATOR CHOMP

While you may not intend to hurt others mentally or physically, you may be at your wit's end. The devil and his minions may have tormented you and coerced you to strike out and be angry with those around you. He wants you to body-slam whatever is in your path. But be aware of the potential consequences and take a breath. Here are some tips for how to let that anger go and respond in an appropriate way.

1. Take notice: Don't let Satan sneak up on you and sack you behind the line of scrimmage. Read the defense and know when he is about to attack. When you feel your anger build up inside, that is the best time to whisper a prayer for grace. "For the anger of man does not produce the righteousness of God" (James 1:20).

2. Commit a verse to memory. Find some verses in the Bible or some favorite quotes related to what's on your mind. When something triggers you, simply recite your favorite verses that give you peace and calmness. Take a look at the book of Proverbs. There are many verses that could help. "Good sense makes one slow to anger, and it is his glory to overlook an offense" (Proverbs 19:11).

3. Think: If time allows, try to step back and examine the situation and circumstances. A spur-of-the-moment decision could have lengthy consequences. "A man without self-control is like a city broken into and left without walls" (Proverbs 25:28).

4. Get enough rest: Exhaustion can lead to a quick fuse. Take good care of yourself and be sure to get enough sleep to give you a clear and sound mind.

5. Exercise and eat right: Shift your frustrations to the gym, and make sure your diet has fruits and vegetables. This will help you feel better. And when you feel better, you act better. "For while bodily training is of some value, godliness is of value in every way, as it holds promise for the present life and also for the life to come" (1 Timothy 4:8).

Throughout your Christian journey, you will face moments when you might be tempted to lose your self-control and temper. One act of anger can put your reputation in jeopardy and provide negative consequences. It doesn't matter if you do this on national television or at home alone. God sees your actions, and He knows your usual way of handling things. Try to keep your emotions in check so you can respond to bad situations in a Christlike manner.

DAY 13
MAKE THE BIG COMEBACK

November 1, 1986: Florida 18, Auburn 17

In him we have redemption through his blood, the forgiveness of our trespasses, according to the riches of his grace. —Ephesians 1:7

Florida junior quarterback Kerwin Bell was hurting. He had missed the two previous games because of an injured knee. But on this day, the Gators were down by 17 points, and the team desperately needed his leadership.

He had come a long way from two years earlier when he came to Florida's football team as a fifth-string walk-on player and had worked his way up to the starting lineup.

This was his time.

The Tigers' pass rush was ruthless, and the Gators could not move the ball. Florida's coaching staff decided to put Bell into the game in the second quarter. The situation was less than perfect. Bell was suffering from an injured knee, and he was rusty from being off for two weeks, but his team was facing a 17-point deficit.

No pressure, right?

But Bell was ready. He completed 17 of 31 passes and fired a 5-yard TD pass to Ricky Nattiel to close the gap to 17-16.

More than 74,500 fans in Gainesville, Florida, were hopeful of a miraculous comeback.

The Gators decided to go for the 2-point conversation and the outright lead. The play was originally designed to be a repeat of the previous score. Bell would pass to Nattiel in the flat. But it wasn't open. Instead, Bell noticed the left side of the field was clear. He decided to run for it, even with a gimpy knee.

"I was just hoping I would get there. It seemed like it took me all day [to get into the end zone]," Bell said after the game about his game-winning 2-point conversion.

The win was monumental.

Bell led a tremendous comeback from 17 points down to give Florida its third consecutive victory and put them at 4-4 for the season.

Meanwhile, Auburn came into the game ranked No. 5 in the nation. The Tigers suffered their first loss of the season and fell out of first place in the Southeastern Conference.

Bell, who was the 1984 SEC player of the year, ignored injury and the insurmountable deficit to lead his team to the enormous upset.

Not many people thought the Gators could do it. But Bell, his coaches, and his team had the confidence to make the play successful.

Have you ever been in a situation where you were mentally or spiritually injured and facing tremendous pressure? How would you respond if the coach put you in the game when your team was down by 17? Would you have the grit and determination to run through the pain and make the score?

In whom we have redemption, the forgiveness of sins.

—Colossians 1:14

TWO BITS, FOUR BITS, SIX BITS, A DOLLAR

Life is tough, and your journey may have its ups and downs. At some point, you might mess up—big. You didn't plan on this, but your choices have consequences. Maybe you made a terrible decision that affected a relationship, or you told a lie about someone that damaged the other person's reputation. Maybe you violated the law and will be facing your day in court. No matter the details of your situation, what is significant is how and when you get back into the game.

THE GATOR CHOMP

You might be down by three scores in the second half, but there is still time to make a miraculous comeback. You may also be injured and have sat on the bench for a couple of weeks. Nevertheless, the coach looks down the bench at you and says, "Get in the game." Here are some ways to be prepared when God signals for you to put on your helmet and get into the huddle.

1. Ask for forgiveness: This is the first step and the hardest one. Disappointment does not feel well, and defeat is even worse. Own your mistakes and take responsibility. Ask the Lord and those you impacted for forgiveness. God is in the business of second chances and new beginnings.

2. Make the change: Learn your lesson and stop the behaviors that led to your mistakes. If you want a different outcome, implement change as soon as you can. Those close to you will need to see genuine and noticeable changes in your actions and behaviors. Place your fear and discouragement at the foot of the cross. "Who gave

himself for us to redeem us from all lawlessness and to purify for himself a people for his own possession who are zealous for good works" (Titus 2:14).

3. Put your regrets behind you: The devil will work hard to remind you of your past mistakes every day of your life. He is the father of all lies and wants to keep you on the sidelines. Use his reminders as motivation to examine the consequences of what you did and strengthen your commitment to never do it again. John Wayne once said, "Looking back is a bad habit." The past cannot be redone, but you can be restored and start a new future today. Don't let your regrets lead to bitterness and depression. Ask God to give you the peace and freedom you need to move forward.

4. Restore your confidence and go after your goals: A setback can injure your confidence. Bell had an injured knee, but he had to get on the field at some point. When you have hope through the Lord, expect to score the go-ahead points. God can give you assurance and equip you with courage. "For I will restore health to you, and your wounds I will heal, declares the LORD, because they have called you an outcast: 'It is Zion, for whom no one cares!'" (Jeremiah 30:17).

5. Follow the Lord: After God forgives you and extends another chance, trust Him as He leads you into battle. The devil will not like that you made the decision to do what's right, and he will try to convince you that you are a failure and should not go for the extra points. Show

Him that you can still cross into the end zone with God on your side.

You can make that comeback even after an injury and setback. The key is to ask the Lord for help to go forward. You only have a couple of quarters left. There is no need to look back. Look ahead to find your receiver for the score and run for the end zone to take the lead.

DAY 14
CHANGE YOUR SHOE

October 29, 1966: Florida 30, Auburn 27

In all things I have shown you that by working hard in this way we must help the weak and remember the words of the Lord Jesus, how he himself said, 'It is more blessed to give than to receive.'"—Acts 20:35

Florida got off to a quick start on this Homecoming Day and took a 7-0 lead after Auburn fumbled the opening kickoff.

Gators quarterback Steve Spurrier, a leading candidate for the Heisman Trophy, fired a TD strike to wide receiver Richard Trapp for the early lead.

The teams traded scores throughout the day, and the Tigers took the lead in the fourth period.

Spurrier, who finished the day with 259 yards passing and completed 27 of his 40 attempts, crossed the goal on a QB sneak to tie the game, 27-27. He then orchestrated a lengthy drive with the game clock winding down.

But the Auburn defense stiffened and forced a fourth down on its own 39-yard line.

A field goal nearly half the distance of the field was a bit out of the range of Florida's regular kicker, Wayne Barnes.

Spurrier was a good athlete and practiced kicking often. He would kick field goals during pregame and make many of them.

He famously waved off Barnes and then changed shoes to kick the field goal himself.

The ball was snapped, and Spurrier put everything he had behind the kick. The ball sailed 40-plus yards and went between the goalposts for the 30-27 win.

The kick not only won the game for Florida, but it pretty much secured the Heisman Trophy for Spurrier. He indeed earned many accolades that year, including the Heisman, the Southeastern Conference Player of the Year, the UPI Player of the Year, and the Walter Camp Memorial Trophy, to name a few.

Spurrier proved he could do whatever it took to win the game. He ran for a touchdown, passed for scores, and even booted his way to a victory.

What can you do to lead your team to success?

For God is not unjust so as to overlook your work and the love that you have shown for his name in serving the saints, as you still do. —Hebrews 6:10

TWO BITS, FOUR BITS, SIX BITS, A DOLLAR

You can do many things for the kingdom of Christ. But are you content to just do the basics? You read the Bible and pray daily. You go to church on a regular basis and treat everyone with kindness and compassion. You have all the bases covered. Right? But is there more you can do? Do you often pass by people less fortunate than you and ignore them? Do you drive by a food bank or a homeless shelter and tell yourself that you will volunteer there "one day"? Or perhaps you have a desire to get more involved in the community and in your kids' lives and activities.

THE GATOR CHOMP

Now is the time to change shoes and line up for the kick. There comes a time to get busy and put your plans into action instead of just dreaming about them. As a believer, you are called to be a representative for Christ. When you wear the Christian label, people will watch what you do for the cause. You are a missionary to your neighborhood. Here are some ways you can be an ambassador for the kingdom:

1. Volunteer your time: Spring into action. Everyone needs recreation and that's fine, but consider making it a priority to help those in need. When God blesses you, pay it forward and spread his love to give them hope. Pick out an organization that helps those who are less fortunate and volunteer your time to make a difference. "If you pour yourself out for the hungry and satisfy the desire of the afflicted, then shall your light rise in the darkness and your gloom be as the noonday. And the LORD will guide you continually and satisfy your desire in scorched places and make your bones strong; and you shall be like a watered garden, like a spring of water, whose waters do not fail" (Isaiah 58:10–11).

2. Use your talents: If you have been blessed with abilities and talents, find a way to use them to honor God. If you are a musician, you might join a praise team. You can make an impact through the unique gifts God has given you.

3. Become involved: Help at church when you can. Be a greeter. Volunteer in the youth ministry. Even to younger kids, you can be a role model.

4. Offer to be a mentor: Volunteer to help your local school by helping at after-school programs. "Do your best to present yourself to God as one approved, a worker who has no need to be ashamed, rightly handling the word of truth" (2 Timothy 2:15).

5. Pray for opportunities: Ask God to open doors for you to walk through and be ready for God to put you into the game that He chooses for you. He might want you to be a prayer warrior or a door greeter. He might want you to serve your pastors or lead a Bible study each week in your home. Be willing to follow His lead and trust His plan for your life.

Spurrier practiced the art of kicking, and it paid off when he booted the ball through the uprights to win the game. Even though this was not his official role with the team, he prepared himself for the opportunity and came through in the clutch. Be prepared to do anything and everything for the cause of Christ.

DAY 15
DEFENSE WINS GAME

September 15, 1990: Florida 17, Alabama 13

Then the Lord knows how to deliver the godly out of temptations and to reserve the unjust under punishment for the day of judgment. —2 Peter 2:9 NKJV

Florida could not move the ball in the first two quarters, and the unranked Crimson Tide was able to take a 10-7 lead into the break over the No. 24-ranked Gators.

Florida quarterback Shane Matthews put together a drive in the third quarter that put the Gators on the board after he found Terrence Barber on a 6-yard TD pass.

But Alabama countered and put together a drive that went deep into Florida territory. Then Gator defensive safety Will White intercepted a 'Bama pass at the 2-yard line. His third pick of the day kept the Gators within 3 points.

Matthews connected with Ernie Mills for a 70-yard play that set the stage for a 23-yard field goal by Arden Czyzewski to tie the game 10-10 late in the third period.

The Gator defense stiffened and forced the Tide to punt deep in their own territory. That's when Florida's Jimmy Spencer bolted through the 'Bama line and blocked the punt by Stan Moss. Richard Fain fell on the ball for the Gators in the end zone to boost Florida to a 17-10 lead.

Three interceptions and a blocked punt kept the Gators in the game long enough to pull off the win over Alabama.

How does your defense stand up to the threats from the forces of evil?

No temptation has overtaken you except such as is common to man; but God is faithful, who will not allow you to be tempted beyond what you are able, but with the temptation will also make the way of escape, that you may be able to bear it. —1 Corinthians 10:13 NKJV

TWO BITS, FOUR BITS, SIX BITS, A DOLLAR

You will be tempted to sin and make mistakes. This is a guarantee in life. As a believer and follower of Jesus Christ, you have a big red target on your back, and the devil takes aim every day. He even tempted Jesus Christ. His enticements come in many forms and fashions—through lust, success, failures, lies, and even good times. Perhaps a coworker makes sure you know she wants more than friendship. A friend may encourage you to try a substance that could lead you down the road of addiction. Maybe you want something you can't afford, so you think about stealing it. You might consider leaving the dinner table at a restaurant without paying because the service was bad. The temptation might look harmless—but this is exactly when you need to play your toughest defense.

THE GATOR CHOMP

Temptation comes at you fast when your defenses are down, and Satan knows all about your vulnerabilities. He will also tempt you when you are on the mountaintop and life is good.

No one escapes temptation on their own, but God always provides a way out if you seek it.

"There hath no temptation taken you but such as is common to man: but God is faithful, who will not suffer you to be tempted above that ye are able; but will with the temptation also make a way to escape, that ye may be able to bear it" (1 Corinthians 10:13 KJV)

Here are some tips to block the punt and make the interception:

1. Recognize and flee: A good defender will recognize when the offense is about to come up with a big play. The key here is to see it before it strikes. Never be so arrogant to assume you are exempt from ever being tempted. Be smart enough to avoid getting caught in a compromising position that will allow the devil to pin you down. Don't try to battle the devil alone. You will not win. The best defense is to get rid of the ball before you get sacked.

2. Have an accountability group: It's easy to change the game plan when you're on your own. But when you play as a team, you are expected to keep your commitments. Who is on your team? Pick four or five people you trust and meet with them regularly in person or talk on the phone. Strive to select people who will hold you accountable and will be honest with you when you drop the pass. This is not a social gathering or a buddy fest. It's a safe place to share your struggles and come up with ways to help each other. Your teammates can also be on call when you travel to make sure all is well. "As iron sharpens iron, So a man sharpens the countenance of his friend" (Proverbs 27:17 NKJV).

3. Have a go-to verse: Commit to memory scripture that has special significance for you to provide encouragement and inspiration when you need it the most. When you get tackled by Satan, recite the verse, and it will provide comfort and assurance. Calling out the name of Jesus is an additional way to make the devil call a time-out.

4. Have a cost card: Make a list of people and things in your life that are valuable and put it in your wallet or someplace where you can access it quickly. When temptation comes your way through lust, drinking, drugs, or gambling, look at the card to remind you what is at stake. You can lose your family, your job, your health, your freedom, and your soul.

5. Pray for strength: This takes self-discipline, but it must be done. Ask God for the self-discipline and the strength to remove yourself from a bad situation. Willingly give your problem to the Lord. If you ask Him to take it, that means you may secretly want to hang on to the behavior. But when you give it away to the Master, you show Him that you really don't want it at all. "For I know that this will turn out for my deliverance through your prayer and the supply of the Spirit of Jesus Christ" (Philippians 1:19 NKJV).

A solid defense will allow the offense to move down the field and score to win. Give way to God's grace and offer up yourself to be a servant so the Lord can take reign of your life. When you continue to flee from temptation, you will get stronger each time. Make the interceptions and block the punt to put the game out of reach.

DAY 16
GO DEEP IN PRAYER

September 20, 1969: Florida 59, Houston 34

Trust in the LORD with all your heart; do not depend on your own understanding. Seek his will in all you do, and he will show you which path to take.

—Proverbs 3:5–6 NLT

No one expected Florida to stay close to Houston, the No. 7-ranked team in the nation. Many experts had the Cougars picked to win the National Championship. The Gators were not ranked and featured many underclassmen on the roster.

But those who did make their way to Florida Field in Gainesville for the opening game had a big surprise waiting for them that day. The estimated 53,000-plus fans were introduced to a group of players that would come to be known as the "Super Sophs."

Florida quarterback John Reaves, a sophomore, threw for 342 yards and five touchdowns. Defensive back Jimmy Barr, also a sophomore, picked off a Houston pass and returned it for a score. And sophomore Carlos Alvarez caught six passes for 186 yards and three TDs.

The Gators rumbled for 502 yards of total offense and thumped the high-powered Cougars, 59-34.

One of Alvarez's touchdowns came when Reaves found his target on a 70-yard bomb on the third play of the game.

Houston, a team that put up 100 points the year before against Tulsa, didn't know what hit them and never recovered.

When Reaves went deep on the third play of the game, it caught the Cougars off guard and set the stage for the upset.

This was a prime example of the importance of being ready for the big game. Are you prepared to meet the Lord? As a believer, you must always be watching for the Lord's return because scripture says that He will come as a thief in the night. Don't be caught by surprise.

> For he has rescued us from the kingdom of darkness
> and transferred us into the Kingdom of his dear Son,
> who purchased our freedom and forgave our sins.
> —Colossians 1:13–14 NLT

TWO BITS, FOUR BITS, SIX BITS, A DOLLAR

Are you in a spiritual battle? Maybe circumstances outside of your control have kept you off your game. Perhaps you have been blindsided by the devil and his offensive line, and this has caused you to second-guess your life choices. You may feel you have trusted God to answer your prayers, but He has not come through in the way you thought He would. Maybe a loved one suffers from health issues, and you are becoming bitter and confused as to why God is allowing them to go through this hard time. The devil schemes to run up the score and take you out of the game on the third play. He tries to distract you by making life too busy for you to pray and read your Bible. If he can divert your focus from what's important, he will be able to block the kick.

THE GATOR CHOMP

When life happens, you may find yourself disconnected from God's presence. A solid prayer life can keep you focused on the receiver sprinting down the field for the score. The forces of evil will throw everything at you to take you out and reduce your playing time on the field. Here are some tips to strengthen your daily walk with God.

1. Be thankful: The Lord appreciates your gratitude. Thank Him every day for the precious gift of life because tomorrow is not guaranteed. If you wake up in the morning, show genuine appreciation for another day you are able to put your feet on the floor and walk across the room. "And let the peace that comes from Christ rule in your hearts. For as members of one body you are called to live in peace. And always be thankful" (Colossians 3:15 NLT).

2. Ask for forgiveness: Tell the Lord you are genuinely sorry for your sins. All we like sheep have gone astray, and no one is perfect. But when we seek God's grace with a humble heart, He will have mercy on us and redeem us from our unrighteousness. No sin is too big for God to handle; His unconditional love is a breath of fresh air in a world filled with evil.

3. Be specific in your prayer: God's Word tells us that we have not because we ask not. Express the desires of your heart to the Lord in detail and be specific. Even though God already knows your needs, He wants to hear about them from you. "Nevertheless, listen to my prayer and my plea, O Lord my God. Hear the

cry and the prayer that your servant is making to you" (2 Chronicles 6:19 NLT).

4. Praise Him: Always give God the glory for the good and for the bad. Praise Him for each day and be thankful even for the things He does not give you because He always knows what is best. You might not have everything you want, but that is by design. God always sees the big picture, and He withholds things for our own good. Some of the dots in His plan may not connect until you get to heaven, but trust Him and realize that He knows exactly what you need today. If you can lift your voice in praise during the dark times, the good times will be even more meaningful. "I will thank the LORD because he is just; I will sing praise to the name of the LORD Most High" (Psalm 7:17 NLT).

5. Limit distractions: Turn off the television and all your electronic devices. It's difficult to stay focused on what God has for when your phone vibrates. He wants your full attention when you go to Him in prayer. Find a quiet place and commune with God.

Life brings struggles to both the saved and the unsaved. But when you go deep in prayer with the Master, you will connect with the receiver sprinting toward the goal and catch the devil off guard. Prayer is a significant part of your Christian journey and is a constant source of comfort and strength. When you pray, you have an open line of communication with the Heavenly Father. Don't let anything come between you and your prayer life. Short passes can chip away at the defense, but the deep pass will bring the crowd to its feet. Make your prayer life a vital part of your daily offense.

DAY 17
DON'T FALL FOR THE TRICKS

October 6, 2018: Florida 27, LSU 19

Now to him who is able to do far more abundantly than all that we ask or think, according to the power at work within us, to him be glory in the church and in Christ Jesus throughout all generations, forever and ever. Amen. —Ephesians 3:20–21

This was a big day for Florida fans. More than 90,000 people packed into Ben Hill Griffin Stadium to watch the No. 22 Gators take on the No. 5-ranked Tigers from Louisiana State. They also were there to watch Tim Tebow be inducted into the Ring of Honor, so emotions were running high for all at The Swamp.

Joe Burrow led LSU to an early 7-0 lead in the first quarter in this old-fashioned slugfest in the Southeastern Conference.

The Gator defense was in full chomp mode and clamped down on Burrow. Coming into the game, the LSU signal-caller had not thrown an interception. On this day, he was picked two times.

Defensive back Brad Stewart Jr. took a Burrow pass and returned it 25 yards for a Florida touchdown with 1:45 to play in the game to secure the win.

But the biggest play happened in the third quarter when the Gators trailed LSU by 6 points.

Head Coach Dan Mullen reached into his bag of tricks and called a brilliant play that caught the Tigers by surprise.

Tight end Lucas Krull took the handoff as he went in motion to the left side of the field. Quarterback Feleipe Franks then darted to the other side of the field, and Krull pulled up to pass the ball. Franks was wide open and hauled in the ball for a 15-yard gain that moved the Gators to the 2-yard line.

Running back La'Mical Perine, who finished the game with 85 yards rushing, scored his second TD of the game on the next play to put Florida ahead, 20-19.

The Gators never looked back and went on for the big 27-19 upset win over their cross-division rivals.

Franks ended the day with 161 yards passing and completed 12 of 27 attempts with one TD.

The Gators controlled the momentum on the field and dominated both sides of the ball.

But it was the trick play that gave them the lead they would never relinquish on the day Tebow was honored.

Have you ever gone into the game as the favorite to win, only to fall to a trick from the devil?

If you are not careful, it can happen before you know what hit you, and it can cause you to fall behind. Stay strong and keep your guard up.

So we do not lose heart. Though our outer self is wasting away, our inner self is being renewed day by day. For this light momentary affliction is preparing for us an eternal weight of glory beyond all comparison, as we look not to the things that are seen but to the things that are unseen.

For the things that are seen are transient, but the things that are unseen are eternal.

—2 Corinthians 4:16–18

TWO BITS, FOUR BITS, SIX BITS, A DOLLAR

Satan does not play fair. He uses every trick in his playbook to surprise you. He not only wants to defeat you, but he wants to run the score up on you as much as he can to try to make your fall even harder. Just when you think life is going as good as it can for you, out of nowhere you are blindsided by a problem you never saw coming. Perhaps you made a decision that distanced you from a friend or a family member. Or maybe you are on the receiving end of some disturbing news.

THE GATOR CHOMP

No matter what circumstance life throws at you, there is an inner strength and peace that only comes through your relationship with Christ. The devil will try to use evil tricks to throw you off balance. Be on the lookout for his wily tactics.

1. Discouragement: One of Satan's most used tricks is to whisper in your ear after a failure that you are no good. He will tell you that you do not make any difference and will suggest that you just give up. It's a trick. "Likewise the Spirit helps us in our weakness. For we do not know what to pray for as we ought, but the Spirit himself intercedes for us with groanings too deep for words" (Romans 8:26).

2. Arrogance: Satan may try to trick you into believing you are invincible. You are too successful and always right,

and you don't really need God. Don't fall for this trick. "When pride comes, then comes disgrace, but with the humble is wisdom" (Proverbs 11:2).

3. Division: This trick is used a lot. Evil minions will cause a rift between you and a friend or start an argument with your spouse that might escalate. He will use friends of your children to influence them to distance themselves from you. Rebellion can be invited and might split a relationship. It's a trick. "Finally, all of you, have unity of mind, sympathy, brotherly love, a tender heart, and a humble mind" (1 Peter 3:8).

4. Temptation: This can come in the form of greed or in the flesh. If the devil can take you out of your game, then he might be able to finish the job and take you all the way down. He's full of tricks. "Watch and pray that you may not enter into temptation. The spirit indeed is willing, but the flesh is weak" (Matthew 26:41).

5. Doubt: Maybe you have had some prayers go unanswered for a while. The devil will try to convince you that God doesn't care or isn't real. It's a trick. You know better. "So faith comes from hearing, and hearing through the word of Christ" (Romans 10:17).

If he does his prep work, a good coach will know the strategy of the other team. The same goes for you as a believer. The devil will try to trick you to make you fall. When you know his game plan ahead of time, you can ask God to help you prepare a strategy that will permanently release Satan's hold on you.

DAY 18
IN ALL THINGS, "CLEVE" UNTO GOD

September 16, 2017: Florida 26, Tennessee 20

Though I walk in the midst of trouble, you preserve my life; you stretch out your hand against the wrath of my enemies, and your right hand delivers me. —Psalm 138:7

Florida needed to come back strong after dropping the season opener, 17-33, to No. 11 Michigan.

The Gators, ranked No. 24, were gifted an extra week to prepare for No. 23 Tennessee after an unplanned hurricane postponed the game, originally scheduled for September 9.

The Volunteers' quarterback, Quinten Dormady, was picked off three times, with one returned for a Gators' touchdown.

Late in the game, Florida led by 3 points when the Vols intercepted Gator QB Feleipe Franks, resulting in a Tennessee field goal to tie the game with only seconds to play.

The game had overtime written all over it.

With nine ticks left in regulation, Franks took the shotgun snap and dropped back to pass from his own 37-yard line. He was forced out of the pocket and eluded a defender. Franks scrambled to his right and saw wide receiver Tyrie Cleveland break away from his defender. Franks reared back and heaved the ball nearly 70 yards in the air in front of more than 87,000 spectators.

The pigskin was in the air for what seemed forever before finally landing in the arms of Cleveland as he went into the end zone for the game winner with time running out on the clock.

A dogpile celebration ensued, and The Swamp was the greatest place in the world to be at that moment.

The "Heave to Cleve" remains one of the most exciting plays in Florida football history.

Have you experienced anything like this as a follower of Christ? Has God come through for you in the last seconds? Do you cleave to God always, or just in a time of desperation?

> But you shall cling to the LORD your God just as you have done to this day. —Joshua 23:8

TWO BITS, FOUR BITS, SIX BITS, A DOLLAR

How is your relationship with the heavenly Father? Is it in the lead, or does it have moments when you fall behind and there are only a few seconds left in the game? Do you only pray and go to church when it might benefit you or your cause? Perhaps you only practice being a believer when you need a favor from the Master.

THE GATOR CHOMP

When you cleave to God, you must separate yourself from the world and cling to the promises of the Lord. All fathers want attention and respect from their children. The Lord is no different. He wants you to be close to Him when times are good and when they are difficult. You should never view Him as a genie in a bottle to grant wishes for you at your command. Here are some ways you can be close to the Lord and hold Him close every day.

1. Fellowship with others: When you spend time with like-minded people of faith, it will strengthen your relationship with God. Iron sharpens iron. If you shine your light for Christ wherever you go, you will meet fellow Christians on the job and in the community. Of course, you can have friends who are not believers, but they are not going to encourage you in your faith. Choose your company wisely and establish relationships with God-believing friends who will be honest with you and inspire you to always do the right thing.

   > Two are better than one, because they have a good reward for their toil. For if they fall, one will lift up his fellow. But woe to him who is alone when he falls and has not another to lift him up! Again, if two lie together, they keep warm, but how can one keep warm alone? And though a man might prevail against one who is alone, two will withstand him——a threefold cord is not quickly broken (Ecclesiastes 4:9–12).

2. Stay active: Attend church regularly. Read and study God's Word and pray every day. Get involved in your church and be a witness for Christ wherever you go. Attend a group Bible study or Sunday School class where you can grow closer to fellow Christians who will pray for you and support you.

3. Serve others: Be a light in your community by giving your time and money to a worthy cause that helps those in need. Take dinner to a family who is hurting or mow the lawn for an elderly widow. Each day we are presented with ways to help others, if we keep our eyes open to be salt and light to others in a dying world.

> Beware of practicing your righteousness before other people in order to be seen by them, for then you will have no reward from your Father who is in heaven. Thus, when you give to the needy, sound no trumpet before you, as the hypocrites do in the synagogues and in the streets, that they may be praised by others. Truly, I say to you, they have received their reward. But when you give to the needy, do not let your left hand know what your right hand is doing, so that your giving may be in secret. And your Father who sees in secret will reward you. (Matthew 6:1–4)

4. Show gratitude: Always be humble and thankful to others for their kindness. Honor your parents, pastors, teachers, and others in authority who love and protect you. Show honor and respect to those you meet. Give thanks to God for His blessings on your life—your family, health, home, food, clothes, and all the comforts of life. Put a song in your heart and focus on the positive things God has given you.

5. Praise God faithfully: When you consistently thank God for what He has done in your life, you separate

yourself from the enemy, and you draw closer to the Lord. Soon you will find yourself wide open in the end zone ready to catch the pass from the Lord. "For it is written, 'As I live, says the Lord, every knee shall bow to me, and every tongue shall confess to God'" (Romans 14:11).

The "Heave to Cleve" is a fantastic way to describe your run with Jesus Christ. He will notice you when you wave your arms to let Him know you are wide open and prepared to catch His blessings. But you must always stay close to Him.

DAY 19
BE IN IT TO WIN IT

November 10, 2007: Florida 51, South Carolina 31

But none of these things move me; nor do I count my
life dear to myself, so that I may finish my race with joy,
and the ministry which I received from the Lord Jesus,
to testify to the gospel of the grace of God.

—Acts 20:24 NKJV

After South Carolina took a 14-13 lead after the first quarter,
there was never a doubt that the Gators would chomp down on
their former coach, Steve Spurrier.

He had won a Heisman Trophy as a Florida player and later
led the Gators to a national title as head coach. Now he was
with the opposing team.

But on this particular day, Florida quarterback Tim Tebow
would play what many experts consider to be an amazing game.
The sophomore signal-caller posted tremendous numbers. He
completed 22 of his 32 passing attempts for 304 yards, and he
ran for 120 yards on 26 carries. At the end of the day, he had
run for five touchdowns and thrown two TD passes for a total
of 424 yards.

Head Coach Urban Meyer said Tebow was worthy of the
Heisman Trophy. "Seven touchdowns. Wow," Meyer said. "That's
pretty good."

Tebow set a career high in passing yards and set a school record for rushing touchdowns with five in one game.

The 81,215 fans packed into Williams-Brice Stadium in Columbia, South Carolina, saw a performance by a player they will likely never see again.

The Florida QB did it all and showed the nation that he showed up to win and would settle for nothing less.

> Therefore we also, since we are surrounded by so great a cloud of witnesses, let us lay aside every weight, and the sin which so easily ensnares us, and let us run with endurance the race that is set before us.
>
> —Hebrews 12:1 NKJV

Are you determined to win in this game called life?

TWO BITS, FOUR BITS, SIX BITS, A DOLLAR

The Christian race resembles Tebow's performance on the field that day. Because of his spectacular season, he took home the prestigious Heisman Trophy, becoming the first sophomore to earn this prestigious honor. This did not happen by accident. He worked hard in the off-season and demanded perfection from himself and his teammates. He was in shape physically and mentally. Are you prepared to play in each game? Are you ready for what the devil will throw at you each day to try to force the fumble? Do you have the faith to keep from throwing an interception?

THE GATOR CHOMP

Each day you wake up to face the enemy. But your strategy to win must be simple—no trick plays or reverses needed. Prepare yourself to run and pass for the scores. Victory requires you to be in the best shape of your life every day. Here are some tips to get your game plan ready to pour it on the devil and run up the score as much as possible.

1. Break the chains that bind you: Know your weaknesses. Satan is aware of them all, and he will use them to try to break you down. If you are an alcoholic, don't walk into a bar. Stay away from things and situations that make you vulnerable. Remove everything from your life that tempts you to sin. Pray to God for rescue and for strength to sustain you as you strive to live a life of righteousness.

> Then they cried out to the LORD in their trouble,
> And He saved them out of their distresses.
> He brought them out of darkness and the shadow of death,
> And broke their chains in pieces.
> Oh, that men would give thanks to the LORD for His goodness,
> And for His wonderful works to the children of men!
> For He has broken the gates of bronze,
> And cut the bars of iron in two.
>
> (Psalm 107:13–16 NKJV)

2. Keep your eyes on the goal line: Tebow scored seven touchdowns in one game. He had his eyes on the targets, and he crossed them to win. Focusing on the goal line will keep you motivated and encouraged. When you see the goal ahead, you become excited for what awaits the victor. After Tebow won the Heisman, he was considered the best player in college football that year. When you are a believer, your prize is a home in heaven, a robe, and a crown. "I press toward the mark for the prize of the high calling of God in Christ Jesus" (Philippians 3:14 KJV).

3. Surround yourself with people who will inspire you to win: Spend your time with those people who will speak life into you, lift you up, and encourage you to do your best. You will always have those who boo from the stands, but hold your head high and keep going. Let God deal with them. You do your part, and He will handle the rest. "Be strong, fear not: behold your God will come with vengeance, even God with a recompence; he will come and save you" (Isaiah 35:4 KJV).

4. Practice, practice, and more practice: Fundamentals are the backbone of success in sports and in your Christian walk. Attend church regularly where you feed on the gospel. Read His Word every day and pray daily. In addition to regular church attendance, look for other ways to worship with fellow believers, such as group Bible studies or Christian concerts. Tebow studied game films of his opponents to prepare for his games, and he practiced daily. You need to be aware of your opponent as well so that you are always prepared to

block the tackle. "Be sober, be vigilant; because your adversary the devil, as a roaring lion, walketh about, seeking whom he may devour" (1 Peter 5:8 KJV).

5. Be serious about your journey: You should never play church just to appease a prospective spouse or improve your image. When you step on the football field, you should want to win the game. Get serious with God, and always give Him your best. After all, He gave His son to die on the cross for you. Make salvation your way of life and serve the Lord with a genuine heart. "A faithful witness does not lie: but a false witness will utter lies" (Proverbs 14:5 KJV).

You won't win every game you play, and the defense might sack you a few times. But when you huddle up with the Lord and let Him design your game plan, you will be sure to win in the end.

DAY 20
CARRY A BURDEN FOR A LOVED ONE

November 29, 2008: Florida 45, Florida State 15

Yet we know that a person is not justified by works of the law but through faith in Jesus Christ, so we also have believed in Christ Jesus, in order to be justified by faith in Christ and not by works of the law, because by works of the law no one will be justified. —Galatians 2:16

The 2008 final game of the regular season became more a crowning than a contest. Florida, ranked No. 4 in the nation, went into Doak Campbell Stadium and thrashed the No. 20-ranked Seminoles of Florida State.

Quarterback Tim Tebow did everything that day. He fired three touchdown passes, ran for 80 yards and a score, and led the Gators to a 45-15 win in rainy conditions.

"I don't know if I've ever seen a better leader," said FSU Head Coach Bobby Bowden. "He's a tremendous player and a tremendous leader."

Not only did Tebow led the team to a huge win, but he also created an iconic image during the game.

The rainy conditions in Tallahassee made the field wet and slippery. In the second quarter, Florida wide receiver Percy Harvin suffered a sprained ankle and had to be helped off the field.

The Seminole faithful cheered when Harvin hobbled to the sidelines. This upset Tebow. After the game he told reporters that he was motivated by their reaction.

"That kind of irritated me," he said. "I told the coach to give me the ball because I really wanted to hit somebody."

Florida Head Coach Urban Meyer listened to his all-star QB and Tebow responded. Not only did Tebow score, but he carried several defenders with him into the end zone. When he emerged from the pile, his white uniform was stained with red garnet-colored paint along with mud and grass because of the wet conditions. He also got paint on his face and helmet, where it remained most of the game.

The picture of Tebow clinching his fists with his paint-stained jersey and mud became a symbol of passion and bravery. He celebrated the score on the sidelines with enthusiasm because he was inspired to take up for his injured receiver.

Tebow carried the burden, and the entire sports world saw him.

The real story wasn't the win; it was how the players supported each other.

What burdens do you carry for your teammates?

Bear one another's burdens, and so fulfill the law of Christ. —Galatians 6:2

TWO BITS, FOUR BITS, SIX BITS, A DOLLAR

Everyone goes through problems and trials. When you act as a friend to those who are hurting and show care for what they are going through, it might help them to deal with the situation better.

THE GATOR CHOMP

As a believer, the Lord calls you to share burdens with loved ones. What does this mean? Human suffering is part of life, and Christ said you should fulfill the law by helping along the way. This doesn't mean you have to get involved and try to solve the problem, but you realize others hurt and you show compassion to help ease the pain. Here are some ways you can make that happen.

1. Give them a phone call or send a text: Personal communication is the best way to let someone know you are thinking about them. You don't have to have a long conversation and ask for all the details, just let them know you are thinking of them. This can be a great source of comfort. Or send a short text telling them that they are in your thoughts. "Blessed be the God and Father of our Lord Jesus Christ, the Father of mercies and God of all comfort, who comforts us in all our affliction, so that we may be able to comfort those who are in any affliction, with the comfort with which we ourselves are comforted by God" (2 Corinthians 1:3–4).

2. Invite them to lunch or coffee: You can always go to the next level and invite them to a meal or coffee, and pick up the tab. Sometimes just getting away from reality for a few moments can be a huge encouragement.

> Then the King will say to those on his right, "Come, you who are blessed by my Father, inherit the kingdom prepared for you from the foundation of the world. For I was hungry and you gave me food,

> I was thirsty and you gave me drink, I was a stranger
> and you welcomed me, I was naked and you clothed
> me, I was sick and you visited me, I was in prison and
> you came to me." (Matthew 25:34–36)

3. Pay them a personal visit: If the person is hesitant about getting out of the house, then drop by with a gift and let them know they are appreciated and thought about. Offer to take them to a movie or for a walk. "A new commandment I give to you, that you love one another: just as I have loved you, you also are to love one another" (John 13:34).

4. Pray for them: This is the best thing you can do to help carry their burdens. When you realize your friend is injured, either mentally or spiritually, you can bring them to the foot of the cross and ask God for guidance and comfort for their weary soul.

5. Send a card or a gift: Send a note of encouragement or inspiration with a gift card for dinner or something they can order online. This can be just the boost they need to get through the day.

Tebow emerged from the pile covered in mud and paint. He carried the burden of his injured player into the end zone for the score. He was motivated to avenge the reaction from the crowd. When you see a friend or loved one who has been hurt, do something about it. Don't gossip or seek revenge but be a friend and show concern. And when the Lord provides a solution, get up and clench your fists together and celebrate the win.

DAY 21
BE DEPENDABLE AND RESPONSIBLE

October 16, 1971: Florida 17, Florida State 15

One who is faithful in a very little is also faithful in much, and one who is dishonest in a very little is also dishonest in much. —Luke 16:10

The No. 19-ranked Seminoles came into Florida Field in Gainesville undefeated with a record of 5-0. On the flip side, the winless Gators (0-5) wanted to salvage something of their rough season so far, and an upset win would do just that.

Florida jumped out to a 7-0 lead in the second quarter but had to punt on its next drive.

Florida State's kick returner attempted to catch the ball, but it popped up in the air after it hit him in the chest. The Gator's defensive back, Jimmy Barr, was alert and grabbed the ball to return it for a touchdown and a 14-0 lead at the half.

Richard Franco added a 42-yard field goal to secure the 17-15 upset win over the rival Seminoles.

Barr was in the right place at the right time, and his team depended on him to make the big play when the opportunity presented itself.

How do you respond when God opens a door for you to a new opportunity? Do you scoop it up and run for the score, or do you stare in disbelief?

Therefore, brothers, be all the more diligent to confirm your calling and election, for if you practice these qualities, you will never fall. —2 Peter 1:10

TWO BITS, FOUR BITS, SIX BITS, A DOLLAR

Acts of kindness happen every day without fanfare or recognition. They may take the form of an impromptu visit to an elderly church member who now lives in a nursing home, mowing the lawn for a friend who is sick in the hospital, or paying for the meal orders for those in the car behind you in the drive-through. Ask God to open the door for you to be of service to others, and don't miss out on the blessing of helping others. Let others know they can depend on you because you are there when it counts the most and do it for the right reason—not to receive a standing ovation but rather to be a kingdom builder for God. A successful athlete or player will gladly take a back seat sometimes for the good of the team. This is good sportsmanship and shows that his teammates come first. You may not receive a reward here on earth, but God has something great waiting for you when you get to heaven. "Lay not up for yourselves treasures upon earth, where moth and rust doth corrupt, and where thieves break through and steal: but lay up for yourselves treasures in heaven, where neither moth nor rust doth corrupt, and where thieves do not break through nor steal: for where your treasure is, there will your heart be also" (Matthew 6:19–21 KJV).

THE GATOR CHOMP

Be the Christian that others can depend on to grab the ball in the air and return it for a score at the right time. And in case you are new to the team, here are some tips to trust God all the time, especially when the ball is high in the air, and you are trying to make the catch in the wind.

1. Surrender all: Give all your wants and needs to the Master. This might sound hard to do at first. After all, faith is easy to talk about, but it can be a challenge under pressure. But once you surrender your cares to Him, He will show you the right route to run to get open for the pass. Get rid of your ego and trust God's game plan. "I appeal to you therefore, brothers, by the mercies of God, to present your bodies as a living sacrifice, holy and acceptable to God, which is your spiritual worship. Do not be conformed to this world, but be transformed by the renewal of your mind, that by testing you may discern what is the will of God, what is good and acceptable and perfect" (Romans 12:1–2).

2. Show gratitude: Try to list one thing you are thankful for each day on a piece of paper. At the end of the week, review your list. You might be amazed at what you see. Those with grateful hearts can be a great inspiration and encouragement to others. "Therefore, as you received Christ Jesus the Lord, so walk in him, rooted and built up in him and established in the faith, just as you were taught, abounding in thanksgiving" (Colossians 2:6–7).

3. Walk and talk with God: Before you focus on your daily tasks, take the time each day to read and study His Word, which serves as your daily playbook. Make this your priority before life starts to get crazy as the

day wears on. This also shows God how important He is to you. Follow up with a sincere prayer to Him, not just the same set of words you repeat each day, and meditate on His goodness to you. Always keep your heart and mind open for what He wants to reveal to you through His Holy Spirit.

4. Put away childish things: If you want to grow in Christ, you need to grow as a person. Parents who provide everything to their teenagers are teaching them dependence and are not helping them to grow into an independent young adult. Work hard for what you have and don't take handouts unless you are in a helpless situation. As a believer, you should have the desire to be like Christ, who was an adult and a mature person. It's OK to laugh and have fun, but you need to be responsible for your actions and get away from being treated like a child. "When I was a child, I spoke like a child, I thought like a child, I reasoned like a child. When I became a man, I gave up childish ways" (1 Corinthians 13:11).

5. Do what is pleasing to the Lord: Paul tells us in scripture that you need to be careful to determine what Christ wants you to do. Your dream in life might be different than what God has planned for you. Be sure to take time to pray and seek counsel from wise church leaders or friends. Seek God's guidance and praise God through everything. You won't go wrong, and He will steer you down the right path. "But I will hope continually and will praise you yet more and more" (Psalm 71:14).

Following this advice can put you in a great position to make the big play. Don't go looking for it to happen, but trust God's plan to put you in the right place at the right time. Always be ready to make the go-ahead play to give your team the lead.

DAY 22
RUN LIKE THE WIND

September 19, 1987: Florida 23, Alabama 14

And he rode upon a cherub, and did fly: and he was seen upon the wings of the wind. —2 Samuel 22:11 KJV

Emmitt Smith made a fantastic impression on his first start as a running back during the 1987 season. The 5'10", 210-pounder broke open a 6-6 tie against No. 11-ranked Alabama on a 30-yard gallop midway through the third quarter. He later plunged into the end zone from 1 yard out to boost the Gator advantage to 17 points.

By the time the game ended, Smith had earned his starting position with 224 yards rushing on 39 carries and two touchdowns as Florida smashed the Crimson Tide. He shattered the 57-year-old rushing record for a first-time starter, previously held by Red Bethea.

The victory was Florida's first over Alabama since 1963 and ended an eight-game losing streak in the series.

Smith's incredible performance would be one of many for Gator fans to watch over his star-studded career as a Florida Gator. Much like the wind, Smith was elusive, and his opponents had a tough time getting their arms around him.

And suddenly there came a sound from heaven as of a rushing mighty wind, and it filled all the house where they were sitting. —Acts 2:2 KJV

TWO BITS, FOUR BITS, SIX BITS, A DOLLAR

Have you ever been in a church service when the presence of the Holy Spirit is moving in a powerful way? It's a tremendous and wonderful feeling. You can feel the Lord moving throughout the sanctuary as people are blessed. Some in attendance make their way to the altar to find spiritual help, and people begin to hug and praise God. Then out of the blue, someone stands up and says something that knocks the wind right out of the service. Just like an Emmitt Smith juke move, the Holy Spirit is ushered out of the building.

THE GATOR CHOMP

Never interfere with the Holy Spirit. Sometimes people pretend to obey the Lord when in reality they are out of bounds. God's Spirit comes where it is welcome and leaves just as fast when there is a lack of discernment. Always be open to allowing the Holy Spirit to move through you, and obey God's commands. When your praise to God is genuine, fellow believers will bear spirit with you in unity. But when worship is done only to be seen, souls are at risk. Do you want to worship the Lord or put on a show? Here are some moments when you could blitz the Spirit of the Lord because your intentions are not ordained, and the wind can get knocked out of a service.

1. When you are angry: If you have a heated discussion with your spouse or a friend before worship, you cannot be an effective ambassador for the kingdom. While it's human to become frustrated, there is a place and time to deal with it, and that's not before and during church. It's difficult to be in a spirit of praise and worship when you are stewing over something. God expects us to arrive at His house ready to receive what He has for us, and He does not get any glory when we don't.

2. When you are bitter: Negativity has no place in the life of a Christian and will not encourage anyone to give their heart to the Lord. Bitterness will fester and lead to resentment and hatred. You cannot feel God's presence when you are focused on resentment. "Let all bitterness, and wrath, and anger, and clamour, and evil speaking, be put away from you, with all malice" (Ephesians 4:31 KJV).

3. When you hold grudges: God tells us in His Word to forgive others. He might even impress on you to do this even when they don't apologize. Giving to God what they did to you frees you to move on to enjoy peace and contentment. C. S. Lewis said, "Everyone thinks forgiveness is a lovely idea until he has something to forgive." Showing mercy to someone who has wronged you is tough, but the freedom it gives you is the best feeling in the world next to salvation. "And be ye kind one to another, tenderhearted, forgiving one another, even as God for Christ's sake hath forgiven you" (Ephesians 4:32 KJV).

4. When you don't live the life of a true believer: No one will respect you if you go to church on Sunday and raise your hands in worship after they have seen you out the night before acting like the world. You are an ambassador for Christ. It's OK to have a fun time out on the town, but it's important to protect your reputation and be the witness God has called you to be all day every day. Be a true example of God's love because eyes are on you everywhere. "He also shall be my salvation: for an hypocrite shall not come before him" (Job 13:16 KJV).

5. When you crave attention: The Lord should be praised, not you. A testimony is your story about how good God has been to you. If all you have to offer are complaints or bad news, stay in your seat and keep your mouth shut. This type of "testimony" doesn't help anyone, and it can kill the spirit in a heartbeat. If what you have to say does not glorify God, you probably shouldn't say anything. "The foolish shall not stand in thy sight: thou hatest all workers of iniquity" (Psalm 5:5 KJV).

Avoid making these blunders and lapses in judgment. Honor the presence of the Holy Spirit and make sure your praise is for real. God will only tell you to do something that will bless others and magnify the name of Jesus Christ. If it won't, then let the wind of deception blow by. Satan comes to church, too, and he will do what he can to knock the wind out of the service.

DAY 23
WHAT'S IN A NAME?

September 12, 1992: Florida 35, Kentucky 19

A good name is to be chosen rather than great riches, and favor is better than silver or gold. The rich and the poor meet together; the LORD is the Maker of them all.

—Proverbs 22:1–2

The Kentucky Wildcats came into a new environment when they visited the Gators at Ben Hill Griffin Stadium in Gainesville, Florida. The fourth-ranked Gators chomped down on the Wildcats and won, 35-19, to open what would become their third straight unbeaten season at home under Head Coach Steve Spurrier.

But the game itself was overshadowed by a new name for their stadium, a name that later took center stage.

Ben Hill Griffin Stadium was the official name of the home of the Orange and Blue. But after this day, it would be forever known as "The Swamp."

This nickname was introduced to Gator fans in a column written by Mike Bianchi and published in *The Gainesville Sun* on June 9, 1992.

His column began:

> "One night, the oldest brother said, 'Ya'll meet me in the Wooly Swamp later. We'll take the old man's money and we'll feed him to the alligators.'" —Charlie Daniels, singing about a place called Wooly Swamp.

> "The Swamp is a place where only Gators get out alive." —Florida football coach Steve Spurrier, talking about a place called Gator Swamp.

The nickname stuck.

Spurrier went on to tell Bianchi that a swamp is hot and sticky and can be dangerous and would be an appropriate nickname for the stadium.

There are many sports venues that also have nicknames. Ohio State has "The Shoe" and rival Michigan has "The Big House."

Florida has "The Swamp," an appropriate name for such an intimidating place for opponents to enter and play.

When others hear your name mentioned, what comes to mind?

> A good name is better than precious ointment, and the day of death than the day of birth. —Ecclesiastes 7:1

TWO BITS, FOUR BITS, SIX BITS, A DOLLAR

A good name is important, and you should strive to be an honorable representative for Jesus Christ. As a believer, you have expectations to live up to, and you must live to a higher standard. This does not mean you are better than anyone else. It means you must live with dignity and integrity—and money has nothing to do with this. Do not leave any room for others to doubt your relationship with the Lord. Set a positive example for others to follow that could persuade and influence them to serve God.

THE GATOR CHOMP

Whether you are a seasoned Christian or a new convert, you represent the name of Christ. Do others think of you as honest and dependable? Or do they have other descriptions that are not as flattering? Here are some tips to maintain a solid and pure reputation of integrity. These might sound like a basic and common sense approach, but they will go the length of the football field to help drive home respect from others.

1. Practice what you preach: Stand on your convictions and make sure they are based on biblical principles. Don't waver from the truth, and always do what is good and righteous. "If a man vows a vow to the LORD, or swears an oath to bind himself by a pledge, he shall not break his word. He shall do according to all that proceeds out of his mouth" (Numbers 30:2).

2. Keep your word: If you make a promise, keep your commitment. When others can depend on you, you earn their trust. Likewise, don't overcommit yourself and set yourself up for failure. Live within your limits but deliver on what you say you will do. "Whoever walks in integrity walks securely, but he who makes his ways crooked will be found out" (Proverbs 10:9).

3. Be a good steward: "Every good gift and every perfect gift is from above, and cometh down from the Father of lights" (James 1:17 KJV). Don't ever take God's blessings for granted. Be ready to give Him the portion He requires. Be honest in all business dealings and pay your debts. You are a representative of Christ, and you don't want to bring shame to His name by skipping out on the bill. You might have to work long hours at times, but be thankful you have a job. Put in an honest day's work and don't short change yourself and God. "The wicked borrows but does not pay back, but the righteous is generous and gives" (Psalm 37:21).

4. Volunteer: Find a charity or organization that supports a cause that is meaningful to you and give it your time and effort. This is a way to give back to your community with humility and compassion. "Love never ends. As for prophecies, they will pass away; as for tongues, they will cease; as for knowledge, it will pass away" (1 Corinthians 13:8).

5. Watch your tongue: Don't fall for the gossip trap. The devil wants you to talk in a negative light about others, but be careful. Avoid telling lies and be careful of the words that come out of your mouth. When you say something bad or incorrect, you can apologize, but you cannot ever take the words back. "Haughty eyes, a lying tongue, and hands that shed innocent blood" (Proverbs 6:17).

When you follow these suggestions, and there are many more, your reputation will grow to become strong and solid. A good name is essential in business and in life in general. But more importantly, someday you want to hear the name "faithful servant," and that won't happen unless you love and protect the sweet name of Jesus.

DAY 24

WHAT KEEPS YOU FUELED?

September 18, 1965: Florida 24, Northwestern 14

And whoever gives one of these little ones even a cup of cold water because he is a disciple, truly, I say to you, he will by no means lose his reward. —Matthew 10:42

The Florida Gators had little trouble disposing of Northwestern at Dyche Stadium in Evanston, Illinois, by a score of 24-14 in front of nearly 34,000 people.

One of the biggest reasons involved the fluid intake of the Gators' players. Instead of becoming dehydrated as the game wore on, the players remained energized because of a new drink. This was because Dr. Robert Cade, Dr. Dana Shires, Dr. H. James Free, and Dr. Alejandro de Quesada developed "Gatorade" for the players to drink.

According to information from Gatorade.com, an assistant coach with the team met with the physicians from the university to find out why Florida players were being impacted by the heat and humidity common in the Sunshine State.

After conducting extensive research, the examiners determined the athletes were losing important fluids called electrolytes through sweating that were not being replaced. The research team also found out the carbohydrates used for energy were not being replenished because of the heat.

The team of doctors, according to the website, went to work and invented a well-balanced drink loaded with carbohydrates and electrolytes that would replace those lost by the players' bodies during competition.

It would aid the Gators and keep them able to perform.

Voilà.

Gatorade!

Florida became known as a second-half team during the season and finished 7-4 in 1965.

The next season, the Gators went 9-2 and beat Georgia Tech 27-12 to claim the Orange Bowl for the first time in the school's history.

Today, Gatorade is a household drink used by athletes all over the nation.

What keeps you going when your opponents wear you down?

> For I will satisfy the weary soul, and every languishing
> soul I will replenish. —Jeremiah 31:25

TWO BITS, FOUR BITS, SIX BITS, A DOLLAR

Has your spirit ever been dehydrated? Have you fallen behind in the second half and found it difficult to keep going? Does your mind get tired of being bombarded by the enemy? You are a target of the devil if you proclaim Christ as your Savior. The game can become difficult at times, especially when you are in the heat of the battle. It can drain your energy and leave you doubled over and ready to collapse. Family struggles or professional obstacles can take a toll on your mental well-being. Satan knows this and will tell you to just give up.

THE GATOR CHOMP

The Lord is aware of the devil's tactics, and He will send the Holy Spirit to help lift you up and restore your strength. He will put the right people in your life at the right time for encouragement when you need a revival in your spirit and soul. But there are also some things you can do to keep yourself hydrated.

1. Use your gifts for the kingdom of God: If the Lord has blessed you with the gift of teaching, singing, reading, writing, or any other special talents, use them to help spread the good news. A spiritual gift does not have to be seen and appreciated by hundreds of people. Perhaps you are a prayer warrior, and no one ever witnesses your gift in action, but they obviously witness the results. As a reminder, God always sees and hears you, and He will reward you when you get to heaven. "For they refreshed my spirit as well as yours. Give recognition to such people" (1 Corinthians 16:18).

2. Be bold: When you trust and believe that God has wonderful things in store for you, then you will have a sense of determination that puts fire in your belly. Take a step of faith by showing courage and trusting that God wants to take you to a new level. This may take some time, so be patient and persistent, and stay ready to walk through the doors He opens for you.

3. Tell others about God's goodness: When you witness or testify about how good the Lord has been to you, you serve as an inspiration to others. Don't save your story just to tell at church but share it with those who are part of your everyday life. It's easy to sing to the choir but

take the challenge and inform those around you that living for Christ is the best life ever. You might be the influence that others need to make the same decision.

4. Be happy: No matter your circumstance, you should always be satisfied within your soul. God has saved you from sin and destruction. Your life may not be what you thought it would be, but take comfort in knowing that you are a child of the King and that He wants the best for you. When you appreciate your blessings, you will be content in life. "Having purified your souls by your obedience to the truth for a sincere brotherly love, love one another earnestly from a pure heart" (1 Peter 1:22).

5. Be of service: When you take time to help those in need, it can provide a much-needed perspective and help you appreciate your current circumstances. Could things be better? Of course. Could they be worse? Yes. Spend some time assisting an organization or take it upon yourself to make a positive impact in your community. Do some lawn work for a widow or rake your neighbors' leaves for them. "For God is not unjust so as to overlook your work and the love that you have shown for his name in serving the saints, as you still do" (Hebrews 6:10).

The research paid off for the Gators. What started out as a remedy to help the Florida players stay strong in the heat led to a wildly successful product that is now sold across the world. With the right attitude, you can have an impact as well and encourage others to want what you have. If you rely on and trust the Lord and stay hydrated in the Holy Spirit, then you can finish the game strong and come out a winner.

DAY 25
WITHSTAND THE STORM

September 16, 1995: Florida 62, Tennessee 37

And as they sailed he fell asleep. And a windstorm came down on the lake, and they were filling with water and were in danger. —Luke 8:23

This was the first major test of the 1995 season. Florida was ranked No. 4 and had crushed Houston and Kentucky to start out the year 2-0.

High-powered Tennessee was ranked No. 8 in the nation with quarterback Peyton Manning at the helm and rolled into Ben Hill Griffin Stadium looking to knock off the Gators.

Manning came out firing and hit wide receiver Joey Kent for a 72-yard gain on the first play from scrimmage. He followed that play with a strike to Marcus Nash for a touchdown and a 7-0 lead in the opening fifteen seconds of the game.

The Gator faithful were stunned after Manning threw for another score. After two Florida turnovers, the Vols held a 30-14 lead late in the second period.

Florida QB Danny Wuerffel had something to say about that. In the closing minute of the half, he tossed a TD to cut the deficit to 30-21.

And this was just the beginning.

A torrential downpour in The Swamp made for the perfect setting.

Wuerffel led a barrage of passes that kept the Volunteers off balance the entire second half. It all started when he threw an 11-yard TD pass to Ike Hilliard, who was Wuerffel's main target the rest of the game with four touchdown catches.

Wuerffel later found Reidel Anthony on an 8-yard TD strike. He then went in from a yard out and concluded the 48-unanswered-point blitz with a twenty-yard strike to Chris Doering.

The Volunteers were helpless in the rain as the Gators went on an amazing run to win 62-37.

The next week, the *Sports Illustrated* cover featured Wuerffel, who threw for 381 yards with seven total touchdowns, even when the weather was bad.

What storms in your life have you played through?

And they went and woke him, saying, "Master, Master, we are perishing!" And he awoke and rebuked the wind and the raging waves, and they ceased, and there was a calm. He said to them, "Where is your faith?" And they were afraid, and they marveled, saying to one another, "Who then is this, that he commands even winds and water, and they obey him? —Luke 8:24–25

TWO BITS, FOUR BITS, SIX BITS, A DOLLAR

How well do you perform in a downpour of rain? Do life's storms bring out the worst or the best in you as a believer? Life can be bright and sunny one day and then drench you with heavy and pounding rain the next. These storms can come out of nowhere and leave you stunned and helpless, much like the Tennessee defense. The gales of life can take many different shapes. Perhaps you are devastated because someone close to you passed away without warning. Or maybe your doctor had to give you some bad news. Or maybe your child stands in need, or your job is on the line. You have two choices when these torrential rains pour: (1) You can give up. (2) You can come up with a game plan and lead an amazing second-half comeback.

THE GATOR CHOMP

Wuerffel's performance didn't just happen by chance. He and the Gators were prepared. Struggles can catch you off guard. If you have the presence of mind to seek shelter and get out of the rain, the damage will be limited and less severe. It will also allow you to put together a plan of attack for the second half. Here are some tips to make sure you are ready to face an unexpected downpour.

1. Stay rooted in the Word: Don't just take comfort in the Bible when times are tough. Find a quiet place to daily read God's messages to you. Stay dedicated to this important daily time, and you will draw closer to the Lord, who will give you the strength to weather the storms.

2. Spend time in prayer: This is your lifeline to Christ. You find time to have conversations with your spouse, kids, colleagues, and friends. Talking to God is just as, if not more, important. This should not be a time to go down a wish list of your wants. But you can share your heart and desires with Him. Set aside time to thank Him for His goodness and salvation. Gratitude should

take priority. God will always be there for you and wants to hear from you on a regular basis—not just when He's your last straw.

3. Sing: When you have a spiritual song in your heart, you will be encouraged to have a positive outlook on circumstances, even when times are challenging. "Let the word of Christ dwell in you richly, teaching and admonishing one another in all wisdom, singing psalms and hymns and spiritual songs, with thankfulness in your hearts to God" (Colossians 3:16).

4. Memorize Scripture: Find a few passages that you like and that inspire you and commit them to memory. When you are soaked with a downpour of rain, whisper the words to yourself. This can have a calming and reassuring impact on you.

5. Praise God: The Master enjoys it when you recognize and honor Him for what He has done for you. Practice praising and worshipping the Lord. When you can do this, it might lessen the storm that you have to go through. "Exalt the LORD our God; worship at his footstool! Holy is he!" (Psalm 99:5).

Wuerffel battled through the downpour of rain to put together a winning performance that Manning could not. When conditions are not perfect, it might be difficult to hunker down and let the storm pass. Sometimes, it might mean you take a direct hit and take on water. But when you are familiar with the Word of God and have committed some of it to memory, combined with singing and praising God, you will have what it takes to endure the blustering wind and rain. Be prepared and ready all the time because you never know when the dark clouds will form over top and rain down on you.

LEARN FROM THE LOSS

November 23, 2013: Georgia Southern 26, Florida 20

These things I have spoken unto you, that in me ye might have peace. In the world ye shall have tribulation: but be of good cheer; I have overcome the world.
—John 16:33 KJV

Georgia Southern was not intimidated by The Swamp as it went into Gainesville and thumped the Gators, 26-20, in front of more than 82,000 fans.

Florida had a tough time defending the Eagles' triple-option offense and yielded 429 of total offense to Georgia Southern.

The Gators jumped out early and took a 10-0 lead after a field goal and a touchdown catch from wide receiver Solomon Patton. At first, it appeared that Florida had the game under control and was cruising to a win in the second quarter.

But before intermission, Eagles quarterback Kevin Ellison scrambled for a 45-yard score that cut the lead to three points.

Early in the third quarter, Ellison ran again for another score to give Georgia Southern its first lead of the game, 14-10.

The Gators rallied and tied the score 20-20 when quarterback Skyler Mornhinweg connected again with Patton for a TD.

But Georgia Southern's offensive attack and triple-option were too much for Florida to stop. Running back Jerick McKinnon crossed the goal line, but the missed extra-point attempt made the score 26-20 with under three minutes to play in the game.

Florida had one more chance but could not connect on passes into the end zone and fell to the Eagles.

This loss embarrassed the team and its fans, and what really poured salt into the wound was the Gators were not going to a bowl game for the first time in ten years.

The Florida defense did not play up to par, and the offense was not what Gator fans had come to expect over the years.

The players were stunned. They knew they could play better, but they did not live up to expectations. Overall, the Gators fell short and posted a 4-8 mark on the year.

Have you ever had a bad season?

Fear thou not; for I am with thee: be not dismayed; for I am thy God: I will strengthen thee; yea, I will help thee; yea, I will uphold thee with the right hand of my righteousness. —Isaiah 41:10 KJV

TWO BITS, FOUR BITS, SIX BITS, A DOLLAR

How do you respond after a tough loss? Although Florida had some wins, the season overall was terrible. But the team rebounded the next year with a 7-5 record and a win at the Birmingham Bowl over East Carolina. The Gators did not stay down. When you have a bad year, the devil wants you to stay discouraged and give up. He wants to slow you down and keep you from reaching your potential as a Christian. He will use hurtful words from others to knock you down or blindside you with a personal problem.

THE GATOR CHOMP

When an unexpected defeat comes your way, it might appear easy to toss in the towel and give up. Satan's demons will try to convince you that quitting is the easiest way out and the best solution. But deep down, you know God expects more from you. He wants you to attack the issues with a positive attitude and the help of the Holy Spirit. He also wants you to pray and stay in the Word—be sure to read the end of Revelation where God wins the game in the end. Here are some other tips to overcome discouragement and learn from a loss.

1. Be honest: Don't make excuses when you mess up. Take responsibility for your sins, mistakes, and bad decisions. You can blame Satan for influencing you to make them, but in the end, you made the choices, and you are accountable. Even solid Christians can make a mistake. Be aware of this and cling to God for comfort and assurance. "Providing for honest things, not only in the sight of the Lord, but also in the sight of men" (2 Corinthians 8:21 KJV).

2. Be vigilant: The devil will come at you when you least expect him to attack. Don't let your guard down and assume you are winning the game when there's still time left on the clock. When he comes at you and knocks you down, then get back up and huddle with the Lord. You have another play to run. "Be sober, be vigilant; because your adversary the devil, as a roaring lion, walketh about, seeking whom he may devour" (1 Peter 5:8 KJV).

3. Stay healthy and get rest: When you are out of shape and don't get enough sleep, you become tired physically and mentally. Satan knows this and will attack when you are the most vulnerable. When you take action to eat healthy foods, stay active, and get the proper rest, your body feels better, and your mind and spirit are stronger. Be sure to stay in shape physically, mentally, and emotionally to be at the top of your game.

4. Seek counsel: If you don't know where to turn, ask God to lead you to the right person to talk to. This may be your pastor or friend. Don't wait before the situation is out of hand, and don't expect others to know you are discouraged. Get help when you need it, but make sure you get it from someone who is for you that you can trust completely. "Where no counsel is, the people fall: but in the multitude of counsellors there is safety" (Proverbs 11:14 KJV).

Everyone gets discouraged after a loss. But Florida's players picked themselves up and came back the next year. In the off-season, the team worked hard and made it back to a bowl game to win a victory. They took the season one game at a time. The key is not to stay down. Lick your wounds but get up the next day ready to take the opening kickoff to the house.

DAY 27
CHASE AFTER YOUR JOY

October 6, 2012: Florida 14, LSU 6

For the sake of Christ, then, I am content with weaknesses, insults, hardships, persecutions, and calamities. For when I am weak, then I am strong. —2 Corinthians 12:10

This game was a good ol'-fashioned gridiron matchup between two Southeastern Conference rivals. The No. 10-ranked Gators got a career-high 146 yards rushing and two touchdowns in the second half from running back Mike Gillislee as they knocked off No. 4 Louisiana State, 14-6, in Gainesville.

The win gave Head Coach Will Muschamp a significant victory in his second season and handed the Tigers their first regular-season loss in nineteen games.

Florida's defense chased LSU quarterback Zach Mettenberger most of the game and held star running backs Spencer Ware and Kenny Hilliard at bay. The Tigers could only convert on one of thirteen third-down attempts.

The Gators chomped down in the second half and scored on back-to-back drives with a potent ground game attack, led by Gillislee.

Florida ran the ball on their final twenty-five plays from scrimmage. But perhaps the most impactful play was a defensive gem. The Tigers were driving in the third quarter. Mettenberger connected with Odell Beckham Jr. on a 56-yard reception. But

Florida's Matt Elam chased down Beckham and stripped the ball from the receiver before he went to the turf.

The Gators took away any momentum from the Tigers and took control of the game to hold on for the win.

Elam did not give up and demonstrated tremendous hustle and effort in the chase for victory.

How hard do you chase the joy of the Lord?

One man of you puts to flight a thousand, since it is the LORD your God who fights for you, just as he promised you. —Joshua 23:10

TWO BITS, FOUR BITS, SIX BITS, A DOLLAR

Although the Gators were down 6-0 at the half, they did not give up. Instead, Muschamp made changes at the break that proved fruitful. What started out as a potential defeat turned into a thrilling victory. Perhaps you have faced some difficult emotions in life and times when it was hard to be happy. Where does your happiness come from? Do you get it from a major job promotion? Does status in your community or a new car do it for you? What happens when the tide turns, and happiness runs out? How do you adjust when life slows down due to unexpected situations? Life can be going great and then go south in the blink of an eye. The fun roller coaster ride might come to an immediate stop and leave you dazed and confused.

THE GATOR CHOMP

Material things should never be the key to your happiness. They can bring temporary satisfaction, but they should not be the main source of your joy. Keeping up with the neighbors is not the best way to keep a smile on your face. Instead, here are some tips to chase joy as it is meant to be experienced.

1. Begin your day in prayer: What better time to spend with God than the beginning of a new day? Try getting up a few minutes earlier to make time to spend with your Creator. Some peace and quiet and alone time with the Lord are tremendous ways to connect and get the strength you will need throughout the day. And a cup of coffee might be in order as well. You can chase the joy He has to offer. "And if we know that he hears us in whatever we ask, we know that we have the requests that we have asked of him" (1 John 5:15).

2. Take a break: Turn off the television, the computer, and the phone, and give your attention to more important things in life such as your spouse, your kids, your parents, and your community. It won't hurt to unplug from social media, and you might enjoy the break. Chase the joy that is out there waiting to be discovered.

3. Write it down: Pick up a nice leather-bound journal and write down what happened throughout the day and how you handled it. You might have experienced something wonderful, or you might record your thoughts about difficult moments. When you take time to reflect, it may have a calming effect. Writing down your thoughts can help you to be honest with God. Add your prayer requests as well, and when those prayers are answered, you can chase the joy.

4. Surrender to God: When situations in life are too diffi-cult to understand and you have done all you know to do, give your trials over to the Lord. Cast your burdens upon Him and give way to the Holy Spirit. When the load is off your shoulders, you can chase the joy. "Little children, you are from God and have overcome them, for he who is in you is greater than he who is in the world" (1 John 4:4).

5. Be positive: Looking for the good in things in all situa-tions will help strengthen your hope and faith. This doesn't mean to be unrealistic, but it simply means to trust in the Lord's power and promise. Encourage and inspire others. Lift them up and give them a reason to aspire for wonderful things. When you give off a sense of hope and positivity, it will be contagious and spread encouragement to others. The only two things you can control are your effort and your attitude. Chase the joy. "And as you wish that others would do to you, do so to them" (Luke 6:31).

When Elam chased down Beckham, he knew something positive was going to happen. He did not give up. He hustled and ran down the opponent from behind to jar the ball loose. His effort inspired his team to win. When the opposing team is ready to make a play to take the wind out of your sails, don't give up. There is joy to be found. You simply have to chase it down.

DAY 28
NEVER FLIP-FLOP

November 27, 1971: Florida 45, Miami 16

Therefore, take up the whole armor of God, that you may be able to withstand in the evil day, and having done all, to stand firm. —Ephesians 6:13

This game was never a contest from the opening kickoff. Florida dominated the Miami Hurricanes in all areas of the game.

Harvin Clark returned a punt 82 yards for the touchdown in the fourth quarter to give the Gators a 45-8 lead at the Orange Bowl in Miami in front of 37,700 fans.

The 1971 season was not the best for the Gators as the team posted a 4-7 record. But quarterback John Reaves was the bright spot in a dismal year.

The signal-caller entered the game 343 yards shy of Jim Plunkett's passing record of 7,544 yards.

Midway through the final quarter, Reaves threw an interception when he was 14 yards away from breaking the record.

With the game out of hand, the Gators wanted to help their QB hit the milestone.

But Reaves was on the sideline watching his defense and the clock wind down.

Miami had the ball on the Florida 8-yard line and lined up to run a play.

When the ball was snapped, all eleven defensive players for Florida flopped down on the field. A confused Hurricane strolled into the end zone for the score.

A sports broadcaster for Miami was stunned.

"The entire Gator defense lies down, letting John Hornibrook go in unmolested," said Morris McLemore. "As it turns out, there was a motive behind the great lay-down."

Indeed. There was a plan.

Reaves trotted back on the field and connected with Carlos Alvarez for a 15-yard pass to break the record.

The "Gator Flop" made it possible for Reaves to reach this important milestone.

But the opponents didn't see it that way. Hurricane Head Coach Fran Curci was upset and did not shake hands with Florida coach Doug Dickey after the game and called the antics by the defense "bush league."

Then after the game, Florida's team added insult to defeat by jumping into the stadium pool to celebrate.

This sparked a rivalry among the players of both teams and the fans.

While the motive for the Gator Flop was well intended, it did not sit well with the Hurricanes.

Have you ever had a good reason to "flop" on your convictions?

Be watchful, stand firm in the faith, act like men, be strong. —1 Corinthians 16:13

TWO BITS, FOUR BITS, SIX BITS, A DOLLAR

What does it mean to take a moral and biblical stand on certain issues? Spiritual conviction is when the Lord convicts your heart about participating in a certain activity or behavior. Where do you stand on gambling away your hard-earned money? Take a good look at what God's Word says: "For the love of money is the root of all evil" (1 Timothy 6:10 KJV). God tells us in Romans 12:1 that our bodies are a "living sacrifice, holy, acceptable to God." Think about that when you are tempted to use harmful substances that will negatively impact your body. The Holy Spirit convicts us to protect us and keep us pure. While you may not think that alcohol in moderation is a problem, consider the many lives and families that have been destroyed when others thought the same thing. If you have a conviction against drinking alcohol, and you are invited to a party where someone might offer you a beer, how do you handle that? Do you stand strong, or do you compromise your beliefs to fit in?

THE GATOR CHOMP

Are your convictions based on the Bible or on society? In today's environment, you are under a lot of pressure to fit in while at the same time putting your words into action. Avoid temptations from the devil to try to get you to flop on what is important to you. Remember, being a Christian is not a popularity contest. It's about being an ambassador for the King of Kings. Here are some important convictions to hold on to when your record is on the line.

1. Truth: You cannot live a lie. You cannot tell a lie. You must acknowledge that God is the creator of the universe. "Jesus said to him, 'I am the way, and the truth, and the life. No one comes to the Father except through me'" (John 14:6).

2. The virgin birth and resurrection: These are the foundation of Christianity. If Jesus was conceived by man, His divinity does not exist, and the Bible is a lie. If you believe that He stayed dead after His crucifixion, then what is your sacrifice for sins? All of God's Word is right and true, and your salvation is in jeopardy if you start cherry-picking the sections you believe.

3. Life: Believers should firmly believe that life begins at conception and ends at natural death. Life is precious in the womb as well as in the nursing home bed. God still loves those who have experienced abortion, and He always stands ready to forgive and heal. This hot-button issue has become extremely political, but neither the courtroom nor Capitol Hill can change what the Bible says: "Before I formed you in the womb I knew you, and before you were born I consecrated you; I appointed you a prophet to the nations" (Jeremiah 1:5).

4. Integrity: If you say one thing and do another, you become a hypocrite in the eyes of your family, church, or community. If you use foul language and tell dirty jokes in the workplace and then glorify God on Sunday, you are not showing the light of a true Christian example in front of others. When your coworkers and friends know you claim to serve God, they will hold you to a higher

standard, and you should too. "A good name is to be chosen rather than great riches, and favor is better than silver or gold" (Proverbs 22:1).

5. Worship and church: Life happens, but events and functions should not regularly take priority over your family or church. There are times when an occasional absence cannot be avoided, but when you start missing because you want to, you are compromising your convictions to be a good example. Attending church gives you fellowship and encouragement to strengthen your walk with Christ, and you will not find this anywhere else. No football player can win unless he shows up at the stadium.

What you believe should be based on the Bible and what God tells you through His Word and the Holy Spirit. There is no justification or wiggle room in certain areas. Take a stand for what is right, and don't lie down on the field to allow the devil to stroll into the end zone.

DAY 29
COME THROUGH WHEN IT COUNTS

September 16, 2006: Florida 21, Tennessee 20

He that is faithful in that which is least is faithful also in much, and he that is unjust in the least is unjust also in much. —Luke 16:10 KJV

The seventh-ranked Gators went into Knoxville, Tennessee, to take on the No. 13-ranked Volunteers in front of more than 106,000 fans. This was a big test for the undefeated Gators in the third game of the season.

Florida jumped out to an early 7-0 lead, but the Vols came back and gained some momentum when they took a 10-7 lead into the half.

Tennessee added to its lead in the third quarter when Montario Hardesty went into the end zone from 1 yard out for a 17-7 advantage.

Florida quarterback Chris Leak rallied the team and brought them to within 3 points when he connected with Dallas Baker on a 4-yard touchdown pass.

But the Vols countered when kicker James Wilhoit nailed a 51-yard field goal early in the fourth quarter for a 20-14 lead.

Leak again rallied the Gators and took them downfield in an attempt to take the lead. But the drive stalled, and Florida was faced with a fourth down and just over 1 yard to go at the

Tennessee 28-yard line. Head Coach Urban Meyer decided to forgo the punt and opted to gamble for the first down.

Freshman backup quarterback Tim Tebow came into his third game of the year at a crucial time. The team huddled up and called the play. Tebow, a 6'3", 230-pound freshman, took the snap from the shotgun formation and rumbled up the middle for a 2-yard gain and the first down. Two plays later, Leak connected with Baker again on a 20-yard touchdown strike for the 21-20 lead.

The Vols had little time left in the game, and quarterback Erik Ainge's pass was picked off by Gator defensive back Reggie Nelson to seal the win.

Both Nelson and Tebow came up big when the team needed them the most.

How do you handle the pressure of a close game?

But whoso keepeth his word, in him verily is the love of God perfected: hereby know we that we are in him. He that saith he abideth in him ought himself also so to walk, even as he walked. —1 John 2:5–6 KJV

TWO BITS, FOUR BITS, SIX BITS, A DOLLAR

Do the clutch plays from Tebow and Nelson describe you? Do you come through when your friends and family need you the most? And even more, can God count on you to deliver when life gets tough and the game is on the line? How will you respond when called on to make a big fourth-down play? Will you be ready to deliver? Or are you prepared to stop the opponent's attempt to win the game with an interception?

THE GATOR CHOMP

Chances are you won't be in a fourth-and-one in the final quarter as a Florida Gator. But you will face challenges in life. How will you respond? Do you have the characteristics needed to help your team win? Here are some traits you may want to consider when you are thrust into the huddle in the fourth quarter and your team needs a first down to stay alive.

1. Be determined: Keep your commitment to the Lord and don't allow anything to deter you in your service to the kingdom. Attend church on a regular basis and let others know how important this is to you. You might be placed in a situation where you are given an option for overtime and extra money, but it means you will have to miss church. God understands that life happens, but be careful to prioritize the right thing. Line yourself up with the Word and make decisions that will glorify Christ. "Strengthened with all might, according to his glorious power, unto all patience and longsuffering with joyfulness" (Colossians 1:11 KJV).

2. Be compassionate: Take the time to show those close to you how much you care for them and that you hurt when they hurt. In addition, make an effort to help those who are less fortunate than you, and never be too busy to lend a hand. "Rejoice with them that do rejoice, and weep with them that weep" (Romans 12:15 KJV).

3. Be available: Put your family's needs above yours. Help around the house instead of playing a video game or scrolling through your favorite social media app.

4. Be bold: If your beliefs are attacked, speak up and give your opinion. If your faith comes under fire, defend it in a kind and loving way that will not result in arguments or ill feelings if possible. Your convictions might bring on ridicule, but you will be respected if you do not back down. Boldness can be achieved without being rude. "And now, Lord, behold their threatenings: and grant unto thy servants, that with all boldness they may speak thy word" (Acts 4:29 KJV).

5. Be grateful: Arrogance should never be a characteristic of a believer. Confidence in who you are in Christ should always take priority. Toss out the ego and be thankful for who you are because, without God's grace, you are nothing. When you acknowledge His power and demonstrate an attitude of gratitude, then you can grow as a Christian. "O give thanks unto the LORD; for he is good, for his mercy endureth for ever" (1 Chronicles 16:34 KJV).

Tebow and Nelson were winners, and they had what it took to lead their team to the win. They were ready to make the big plays when their team needed them the most. Godly leadership can put you in a situation where you come out victorious and give your team a much-needed win.

DAY 30
EXPECT THE UNEXPECTED FROM GOD

December 2, 2006: Florida 38, Arkansas 28

I will recount the steadfast love of the LORD, the praises
of the LORD, according to all that the LORD has granted
us, and the great goodness to the house of Israel that
he has granted them according to his compassion,
according to the abundance of his steadfast love.

—Isaiah 63:7

The No. 4-ranked Gators had their hands full. They were
playing No. 8-ranked Arkansas in the Southeastern Conference
Championship game at the Georgia Dome in Atlanta in front of
more than 73,000 fans.

A Florida win would enhance their chances of playing for
the National Championship, especially since the second-ranked
Trojans of USC had lost to UCLA that same day. Both the
Gators and Razorbacks were looking to capture the SEC crown
for the first time in several years.

With a 3-0 lead in the second quarter, Florida quarterback
Chris Leak scampered in the end zone on a keeper for a touchdown. Leak followed that play with a 37-yard TD strike to wide
receiver Percy Harvin to increase the lead to 17-0.

Arkansas responded and QB Casey Dick tossed a 47-yard
pass to Marcus Monk to make the score 17-7 at the break.

The Razorbacks came out in the third quarter with a mission, and a different look—the wildcat formation. Running back Darren McFadden acted like he was going to run the ball, but he pulled up and threw a 2-yard touchdown pass to Felix Jones.

On Florida's next drive, Leak attempted a shovel pass that was picked off by Arkansas defensive player Antwain Robinson, who took the ball to the house for the stunning 21-17 lead.

After each team traded possessions, the Gators were forced to punt. But the Razorbacks punt returner, Reggie Fish, muffed the catch when he tried to haul the ball in over his shoulder near the goal line. Freshman Wondy Pierre-Louis pounced on the ball in the end zone for the Gators and the 24-21 lead.

Game MVP Harvin, a freshman, gave the Gators a 10-point lead when he bolted through for a 67-yard touchdown.

The Razorbacks countered when receiver Cedric Washington threw a 29-yard touchdown pass to Jones on another trick play.

Florida had a 3-point lead, and Head Coach Urban Meyer knew that was not enough to win the game. Leak led a drive all the way to the Arkansas 5-yard line. Meyer sent freshman sensation Tim Tebow into the game. By this time in the season, defensive coaches knew he was hard to stop near the end zone and often used his 6'3", 230-pound frame to bully his way over the goal line.

But not this time.

Tebow appeared to be headed toward the end zone when he pitched the ball to wide receiver Andre Caldwell, who pulled up and threw a TD pass to tight end Tate Casey for the 10-point lead.

Florida won the SEC Championship and went on to defeat Ohio State in the BCS National Championship Game.

For he said, "Surely, they are my people, children who will not deal falsely." And he became their Savior.

—Isaiah 63:8

Life is full of unexpected events. Do you worry when these happen, or are you excited to see how God works them out?

TWO BITS, FOUR BITS, SIX BITS, A DOLLAR

Life sometimes involves trick plays that you aren't ready to handle. Maybe your career takes an unusual turn, or a long-time friend turns on you for something you didn't even do. Your circumstances may not be what you envisioned, so you begin to question God. Why are you facing trials when others around you appear to be happy and carefree?

THE GATOR CHOMP

One of the hardest parts of being a Christian is waiting on the Lord. In John 11, some were intrigued as to why Jesus waited four days to go see Lazarus after he found out he was sick. What was He waiting on? After all, Lazarus was dead by the time He and His disciples got there. Everyone thought He was too late, but His timing was perfect, and He was able to demonstrate the power of God by bringing Lazarus back to life. Just when you might think all hope is lost, the Master can show up and take care of your problems in His own perfect way and time. But when he doesn't show up when and how you thought He should, how do you respond? Here are some scenarios when you can expect the unexpected from God.

1. When you don't understand: Have you ever asked, "How could God let this happen to me?" Maybe you serve Him and do all the right things, and something happens that makes you question God's love for you. It's normal to question, especially if your life has been turned upside down. But the devil always fights harder when he's about to lose, so this is the time to get excited and trust God that something big is about to happen. His plans are always good and better than anything you could have dreamed up yourself. Expect the unexpected. "When you did awesome things that we did not look for, you came down, the mountains quaked at your presence" (Isaiah 64:3).

2. When you are afraid: Fear is a powerful motivator. No one wants to fail or lose, but it will happen. Be still and know that God wants the best for you. He tells you in Jeremiah that He wants a good future for you full of hope. Christ will deliver for you—in His time and His way. Expect the unexpected. Hope in God will take away your fear and help you trust in God's goodness and His grace.

3. When you wait: Waiting is hard. In today's society of fast food, the internet, and 24-hour news, everyone seems to have a short attention span and wants things NOW. But even God has a sense of humor, and He might make you wait on His timing to see how you will respond or to teach you patience. God takes nine months to create a newborn child in the womb, and all farmers and gardeners know the importance of waiting for their planted seeds to take root and grow.

The outcome, God's beautiful creation, is worth the wait. Expect the unexpected. "Wait for the LORD; be strong, and let your heart take courage; wait for the LORD!" (Psalm 27:14).

4. When you can't figure it out: When you are faced with options beyond your scope of thinking, turn your problems over to the Lord. When you don't know what to do, go deep in prayer and in the Word of God. He will place you in situations to teach you to trust Him. Expect the unexpected.

5. When it's too late: The big promotion might have passed you by, or the relationship you thought was "the one" fizzled out, and now you feel that time is working against you. When God closes the door to something that you thought was best for you, you will find out that He had something better in mind. When the Lord shows up, you will see that He really knew what He was doing all along. Expect the unexpected.

No one expected all the trick plays throughout the game. The Razorbacks expected Tebow to push through the defensive line for the TD, but he threw them off when he pitched the ball. The play caught them all by surprise and resulted in a Florida score to secure the win. The devil will pull his tricks to throw you for a loop, but God has His own strategy to take Satan out of the picture. Just trust and expect Him to do the unexpected.

DAY 31
THE GOAL-LINE STAND

November 19, 2016: Florida 16, LSU 10

Pay attention to yourselves! If your brother sins, rebuke him, and if he repents, forgive him. —Luke 17:3

This rivalry between Florida and LSU was supposed to be played in The Swamp in early October, but it was postponed because of Hurricane Matthew. The Category 5 hurricane forced millions of Floridians to evacuate, caused nearly $3 billion in damage in the state, and twelve of the forty-seven people who died were Floridians.

After much debate, officials with the Gators gave in to the demands of the Tigers' athletic director, who insisted on playing a home game in November. Some speculated that Florida was afraid to come to Tiger Stadium. Gators Head Coach Jim McElwain denied the allegations and agreed to make the trip.

Southeastern Conference officials got involved and said that neither team would be eligible for the conference title if they did not play at least eight conference games in the season.

The game was set, but there was some ill will in the air. The first half was a defensive struggle on both ends, and LSU took a 7-3 lead into the half.

The Tigers had a chance to increase the lead in the third quarter but botched a field goal attempt on the Florida 5-yard line.

Florida wasted no time, and quarterback Austin Appleby connected with freshman Tyrie Cleveland on a 98-yard touchdown play that gave them the 10-7 lead.

The Tigers countered with a field goal to tie the game 10-10.

Two Gator field goals put them up 16-10, but McElwain knew deep down he needed more points to win.

LSU had one last drive to either tie or win the game. They moved the ball downfield and had a first-and-goal at the Florida 7-yard line with fifty seconds left in the game.

There was excitement on the LSU side and fading hope for the Gators. The Tigers made it to the 1-yard line and with enough time for two more plays.

Third down came. No gain.

Fourth down. Gators defensive back Marcell Harris and lineman Jordan Sherit stuffed LSU's Derrius Guice inches away from the goal line to secure the win.

They did it! A tremendous goal-line stand against rival LSU secured the win, and a huge celebration ensued in the Tiger end zone.

The Gators made it to the SEC title game, where they lost to Alabama.

But against the Tigers, Florida did not give in under pressure.

Does this describe you?

But avoid foolish controversies, genealogies, dissensions, and quarrels about the law, for they are unprofitable and worthless. As for a person who stirs up division, after warning him once and then twice, have nothing more to do with him, knowing that such a person is warped and sinful; he is self-condemned.

—Titus 3:9–11

TWO BITS, FOUR BITS, SIX BITS, A DOLLAR

As a believer, you will face moments when your faith and convictions are put to the test. Major storms of life can change your plans and leave you in a compromising position. The Gators found themselves in a situation they did not choose, but they did what they had to do to win. You might be bullied or made fun of by people who hate the cause of Christ. There might be times in your life when you will have to make a choice to stand up for the gospel or to blend in with the secular culture. Will you make a goal-line stand?

THE GATOR CHOMP

God did not promise you easy games. Life is tough, but make your presence known and stand up for Christ, even when it's not popular. You can do this in a bold fashion and tell everyone around you that you will not be scored on in the final seconds. Here are some ways to witness to others and make sure they know what team you are on.

1. Read your Bible in public places: It's a good idea to have your own quiet place for your daily devotions, but it doesn't mean that's the only place you can read God's Word. If you are waiting in an airport or on the plane, take it out and read His love letter to you. Keep it in your backpack and take it out for a Bible study at a coffee

shop. Don't be afraid to read your playbook in front of the other team.

2. Serve others: Be active in the community and demonstrate a servant's heart. Put yourself on the front lines. This will give you a compassionate heart and a boldness to not back down. "Religion that is pure and undefiled before God the Father is this: to visit orphans and widows in their affliction, and to keep oneself unstained from the world" (James 1:27).

3. Invite others to the house of God: When your coworkers invite you to a party, return the favor and tell them about your regular church services, a revival meeting, or other special church events they might want to attend. Take a stance and extend a hand to welcome newcomers into the fold.

4. Talk openly about your faith: You can do this without being annoying. Bring up God's goodness in conversation with humility. If you are asked about your weekend, mention going to church with your family to hear a fantastic sermon. Let them know if anyone gave their hearts to Christ. You can work it into the conversation. Take a chance.

5. Be approachable with those who disagree with you: If a person challenges your faith and disagrees with your beliefs, listen to them, and don't argue. Hear them out. Acknowledge their concerns and address them with love and compassion. Be prepared to share your faith. Know your Bible, and be sure to prioritize your daily devotions, prayer, and church attendance. This

will strengthen you to take a goal-line stand against your opponents. "Proclaiming the kingdom of God and teaching about the Lord Jesus Christ with all boldness and without hindrance" (Acts 28:31).

The Gators played an unscheduled game in the opponent's stadium. They were in an unfriendly atmosphere, but they came out a winner. They were prepared and didn't back down. You too can possess the boldness and love of Christ to send a message that your faith will not be defeated.

DAY 32
YOUR REWARD

December 8, 2007: The Heisman Trophy

Do all things without grumbling or disputing, that you may be blameless and innocent, children of God without blemish in the midst of a crooked and twisted generation, among whom you shine as lights in the world.

—Philippians 2:14–15

What a season. Tim Tebow's sophomore year at Florida's quarterback position was amazing.

At first, there was a lot of negative speculation about his skill set as a passer. In the first game against Western Kentucky, he completed 13 out of 17 attempts (76 percent) for 300 yards and three touchdowns.

After that, all the second-guessing of Coach Urban Meyer's selection disappeared.

The 6′3″, 230-pound signal-caller ended the regular season with the second-highest passing efficiency in the nation at 177.8. And he was also remarkable on the run with an average of 4.3 yards per carry.

During the 2007 campaign, Tebow set several university records:

➢ Total touchdowns in the SEC with 55

➢ Single-season rushing touchdowns with 5, Nov. 10

> ➤ The most rushing touchdowns in SEC with 20

> ➤ Most rushing yards in a single game by a Gator QB
> with 166

In the game against Florida State, Tebow threw for three touchdowns and ran for two as the Gators blew out the rival, 45-12. During the game, he fractured his right hand in the third quarter but refused to come out of the contest. For the next three games, he had to wear a cast while he played.

He was by far the best player in the nation as well as the team's leader. He won First Team All-SEC honors and was a First Team All-American selection. He received the Davey O'Brien Award presented to the best quarterback in the country and many other accolades.

But on December 8, he was given the most prestigious award in college football. Tebow earned the Heisman Trophy and became the first sophomore ever to win the award presented to the most outstanding football player of the year.

The voting was not even close. He received 462 first-place votes for 1,957 points. The runner-up was Arkansas running back Darren McFadden, who got 291 votes.

Tebow was the only player in the history of the FBS to pass and rush for at least twenty TDs. In all, he threw for thirty-two touchdowns and rushed for twenty-three. He joined Steve Spurrier and Danny Wuerffel to win the Heisman while a quarterback at UF.

What prize can you earn as a follower of Christ?

For even when we were with you, we would give you this command: If anyone is not willing to work, let him not eat. For we hear that some among you walk in idleness, not busy at work, but busybodies. Now such persons we command and encourage in the Lord Jesus Christ to do their work quietly and to earn their own living. —2 Thessalonians 3:10–12

TWO BITS, FOUR BITS, SIX BITS, A DOLLAR

If you are a true believer in Jesus and your sins are under the blood, then you will be rewarded with everlasting life in heaven. This is enough to excite anyone. But does that mean you coast by and reap the benefits of God's sacrifice? Not at all. You are called to do more. You have an obligation to tell others about the goodness of the Lord and to be an impactful representative of the gospel.

THE GATOR CHOMP

But what can you do? What will be your reward? Will the Lord give you special privileges in heaven? Will your mansion be bigger than those who do not work as hard as you? Of course not. But there are some things you can do to receive God's favor while on earth. Here are a few suggestions.

1. Show compassion: Everyone is susceptible to failure, and nobody is perfect. Even those you may look up to as role models can have moments of weakness. Reach out to those who are less fortunate than you either financially or emotionally. If you see people in your church or community who are in need, do your best to help

them. God will bless you for showing compassion and helping your brothers or sisters in Christ. "The steadfast love of the LORD never ceases; his mercies never come to an end; they are new every morning; great is your faithfulness" (Lamentations 3:22–23).

2. Give with a generous attitude: The Bible says to tithe at least 10 percent of your wages unto the Lord. But you can do even more for the cause of Christ by giving extra to missions and charities above and beyond your obligation to your home church. God blesses those who bless others. If you struggle to make ends meet, then reevaluate your priorities. Are you being a good steward of the money God has given you? Are you tithing regularly? Are you overwhelmed with debt? Put your finances in God's hands, and don't buy things you can't afford. Your reward is in heaven and not on earth, and when you leave this earth, you cannot take any material items with you. If you have been blessed, then consider sacrificing to help a person in need. Do you really need those new golf clubs? Or would it be better to help feed some elderly people in your church? Put your money to good use for the kingdom of God.

3. Get involved: Don't sit on the sidelines and just watch others play the game. Tebow played with a fractured hand because of his desire to win. Jump in and get involved. If you like to drive, then volunteer to drive for your church's bus ministry. If you have a knack for cleaning, then stay after service and help the custodians. Help outside your church by helping out community organizations that are helping others.

4. Be honest: Give your church, family, and employers an honest effort in all you do. "The integrity of the upright guides them, but the crookedness of the treacherous destroys them" (Proverbs 11:3).

5. Fast, pray, and read: Sacrifice something important to you, such as a meal or a day out on the lake, and spend it with the Lord in prayer. He sacrificed His son for you. The least you can do is give up something you love once a month. Spend time on your knees and in His Word. Good things will happen, and you will be rewarded for your efforts.

You may not receive a big Heisman Trophy, but you could be on the receiving end of a hug from a widow whose grass you mowed. Or someone might send you a gift card to take your spouse out to dinner. Make a point to help others without expecting something in return. It's nice when someone shows gratitude, but this should not be your purpose for helping. The best reward you will receive from the Lord is peace and a heart full of love.

DAY 33
DO WHAT IS BEST FOR YOUR TEAM

September 17, 1977: Florida 48, Rice 3

Everyone who is arrogant in heart is an abomination to the LORD; be assured, he will not go unpunished.

—Proverbs 16:5

Cris Collinsworth was a standout high school athlete and attracted the attention of many college recruiters. He was tall, thin, and fast—an all-American high school quarterback.

Collinsworth was best-known as the three-time Pro Bowl wide receiver for the Cincinnati Bengals and pulled down 417 catches for more than 7,000 yards in the NFL.

But when he was offered a scholarship by Florida Head Coach Doug Dickey, Collinsworth accepted as a quarterback.

The coaching staff was excited about the possible option offense that Collinsworth could lead.

In the 1977 season opener against Rice, the game was a blowout. Collinsworth was a third-string QB and got the chance to play in the fourth quarter. His first pass as a Gator was an NCAA record-setting 99-yard touchdown to Derrick Gaffney.

During the season, the Gators were led by Terry LeCount under center. The option offense struggled, and the coaching staff decided to move Collinsworth to wide receiver.

The 6′5″, 180-pound freshman flourished in the new role. By the end of the following year, he had earned First Team All-Southeastern Conference honors. This happened again in 1979 and 1980. He also was a First Team Academic All-American in 1980.

He was named captain his senior year and led the Gators to an 8-4 record and was named the MVP of the 1980 Tangerine Bowl.

During his four years in Florida, Collinsworth caught 120 passes for 1,937 yards with fourteen touchdowns. He also added two rushing TDs, one from a kickoff return, and he threw two TD passes.

The Bengals selected him in the second round of the NFL Draft in 1981. In 1991, Collinsworth was inducted into the University of Florida Hall of Fame.

Would Collinsworth have enjoyed such a wonderful career in college and the NFL if he had stayed at the quarterback position? No one will ever know. But he put his first love of playing quarterback aside his freshman year and did what his coaches needed him to do.

As it turned it, the move helped him and his team.

Can you put aside your best interests in order to do what is best for your team? Or do you insist on doing things your way?

I can do nothing on my own. As I hear, I judge, and my judgment is just, because I seek not my own will but the will of him who sent me. —John 5:30

TWO BITS, FOUR BITS, SIX BITS, A DOLLAR

Many people do things in life they never thought they would do. I have a friend who spent years working in the financial markets and was not happy. In his fifties, he told me that God called him to buy and run a professional racing team. That sounded exciting except he knew nothing about racing. He listened to God and put aside what he wanted to do. It was scary but fun, and he now enjoys a wonderful business and glorifies the Lord with his venture. Could you do this? Would you put your plans on the back burner if Christ wanted you to make a big move?

THE GATOR CHOMP

If you are not willing to trust the Lord to guide your future, then you won't experience the Lord's peace and contentment. If you are struggling with a move that Jesus wants to make for you in your life, true obedience will bring happiness. If not, you might encounter the following issues.

1. Bitterness: When you fight God's will for your life, the Holy Spirit will convict you and urge you to submit to His calling on your life. Don't let your stubbornness make your heart grow hard. Repent and make His will your will and kick your ego through the uprights. If you don't, you could become miserable and full of bitterness. Allow God to change your plans.

2. A lousy attitude: You must do what is needed for your team to win. If you go your own way and don't let God make the play calls, your team will never win. Healthy competition is good, but you have to follow the game

plan. You might be faced with turning down a promotion at work so you can stay with friends and your church. Make sure your final decisions involve huddling in prayer and taking into account what is best for all involved.

3. Stubbornness: It's hard to admit when you're wrong, and you can become increasingly bull headed and uncaring about the views of others. Pride keeps you from admitting you are wrong or that you've made a mistake. But God still loves you, and He may lead you to a divine reversal. Remember what He did when Jonah disobeyed His call to go to Nineveh. While you may not end up in the belly of the whale, God definitely has creative ways of getting what He wants. You might as well just give in to His plan for your life.

4. Selfishness: Be aware that the choices you make in life do not just affect you—they affect family and friends. If you are out of the will of God, those close to you will know it when you become difficult to be around. In addition, you prevent them from living a blessed life as well. Life is good when you're on God's side and obeying His plan for your life. It doesn't necessarily mean you are rich, but peace with God is what really matters. Don't make your loved ones pay for your sin and disobedience. "Let no one seek his own good, but the good of his neighbor" (1 Corinthians 10:24).

5. Negativity: Don't live in the past. Just because something was good before does not mean you cannot change and do something different if God asks you to. When you disobey God, you will gain a miserable

bulls-eye view of the rest of your world. Your marriage is now dull. Your church is too small. Your family is annoying. You will drive away your friends who might be able to encourage you to do the right thing. Follow God's will for your life, and suddenly the world seems right again. Make the change for the betterment of the team. "I can do all things through him who strengthens me" (Philippians 4:13).

The quarterback is a high-profile position and gets the most attention on a team. But Collinsworth was asked to give that up and change positions at a crucial time. He listened to his coaches and made the switch. He could have refused, but he made the choice to do what was best for his team, and at the end of the day, it was a great choice for him too. God will bless those who stay in the center of His will and follow His plans for their lives.

DAY 34
INSPIRE THE DRIVE

November 7, 1970: Florida 24, Georgia 17

But the Helper, the Holy Spirit, whom the Father will send in my name, he will teach you all things and bring to your remembrance all that I have said to you.

—John 14:26

The Bulldogs had a 17-10 lead in the final quarter and were about to score on Florida in Jacksonville, Florida. But Gator linebacker Jack Youngblood stopped Georgia running back Ricky Lake in his tracks, jarred the ball loose, and pounced on the pigskin on the 1-yard line.

From there on, it was all Florida.

Gator Head Coach Doug Dickey turned quarterback John Reaves and wide receiver Carlos Alvarez loose. With just over five minutes to play in the game, the duo connected on a 32-yard touchdown strike to tie the game, 17-17.

Georgia turned the ball over on downs when Florida's Robert Harrell smashed Bulldog quarterback Paul Gilbert at the line of scrimmage on a fourth-down-and-one near midfield.

Reaves then connected with Alvarez on the right side of the field at the Georgia 15-yard line. Alvarez avoided the defensive back and scampered into the end zone for the game-winning score.

The win gave Dickey his first victory over rival Georgia and ended a two-year win streak over Florida.

It also increased the Gators' record to 13-5-1 against the Bulldogs since 1952.

The come-from-behind victory was inspired by the magnificent play made by Youngblood. Without the hit-and-fumble recovery, the next two touchdown drives might not have happened.

Youngblood's aggressiveness prevented a certain score from Georgia and gave the Gators new life with just enough time for the comeback.

Have you ever come through at the last minute to inspire a comeback?

The Spirit of the Lord GOD is upon me, because the LORD has anointed me to bring good news to the poor; he has sent me to bind up the brokenhearted, to proclaim liberty to the captives, and the opening of the prison to those who are bound; to proclaim the year of the LORD's favor, and the day of vengeance of our God; to comfort all who mourn. —Isaiah 61:1–2

TWO BITS, FOUR BITS, SIX BITS, A DOLLAR

A lot of people might count on you. Know that your parents always want you to do good, and hopefully you want to make them proud. In today's world, young people often put athletes and entertainment stars on a pedestal, always checking their social media posts and buying their branded products. But you can be an inspiration too. There are eyes that watch you more than you realize. They may be your kids, friends, family, or coworkers. You have an influence on everyone around you, and you have the ability and platform to inspire someone to make a comeback.

THE GATOR CHOMP

You don't have to be a linebacker to inspire a person to greatness. You don't have to be a preacher or a singer to influence those in your circle. You don't have to be a leader or an employer for a major company either. All you need to be is compassionate, humble, grateful, kind, and positive. If you want to inspire someone, stand ready to accept your role as a follower of Christ. You can accomplish this goal by doing the following:

1. Read and pray: Let your family see you read God's Word and learn scripture to share with them when they need it. Make sure they know you pray for them every day. Establish a weekly devotion time that fits your family's schedule and have each member take a turn at leading.

2. Be present: You cannot win a football game if you do not show up to play. If your children have functions or games after school, make sure you are there. If you have a conflict with your job or a meeting, that's OK. But don't volunteer for overtime or schedule an appointment on purpose when you know your kids depend on your support. Be there for their special days and turn off your phone when you spend time with them one-on-one.

3. Share your talents: You have a gift. Find it. God has placed something within you that He intends for you to share. If you don't know what it is, then pray and ask

God to show you. Keep in mind it may be something that is not seen by everyone. Your talent might be sending out cards to those folks you know who are sick or raising a garden to give away food. Your gift can inspire others. "Having gifts that differ according to the grace given to us, let us use them: if prophecy, in proportion to our faith" (Romans 12:6).

4. Be involved: Take part in the lives of your loved ones. "Remember your leaders, those who spoke to you the word of God. Consider the outcome of their way of life and imitate their faith" (Hebrews 13:7).

5. Be responsible: Become a leader in your home and community. Be a role model wherever you go, and know that others are always watching, so be careful where you go, and make sure the words that come out of your mouth do not offend anyone. "For the one who sows to his own flesh will from the flesh reap corruption, but the one who sows to the Spirit will from the Spirit reap eternal life" (Galatians 6:8).

Youngblood was a standout defensive player for Florida. The play he made midway through the final quarter was just what the Gators needed to inspire the offense to come from behind. You can do the same thing. Step up in the hole and recover the fumble. Then sit back and watch those around you do great things.

DAY 35
WHAT IS YOUR SCORE?

August 30, 2008: Florida 56, Hawaii 10

But thanks be to God, who gives us the victory through our Lord Jesus Christ. —1 Corinthians 15:57

This lopsided win over Hawaii was just the beginning.

Maurkice Pouncey started as the full-time center for Florida in his sophomore year. He was blessed to play next to his brother, Mike, who was the right guard on the offensive line.

As a freshman the year before, Maurkice had seen action at both guard and center. The 6'4", 304-pounder became the seventh freshman to start in Florida history. He had six games during the season in which he earned a grading score of 90 percent or better.

In the third game of the season against Tennessee, he earned a score of 93 percent. Three weeks later, he was selected as the Southeastern Conference Offensive Lineman of the Week.

Against LSU, he was graded at 97 percent and at a near-perfect 98 percent against Kentucky.

The Gators went on to win the SEC Championship and knock off Oklahoma to capture the FedEx BCS National Championship trophy.

The next season, on October 10, the Gators went to Death Valley to face No. 4 LSU. Pouncey posted a season-high grade of 99 percent in the 13-3 win over the Tigers.

His twenty-eighth straight start would be his last at The Swamp.

He racked up several awards and entered the NFL Draft after his junior year. The Pittsburgh Steelers took him in the first round, and he went on to win numerous honors with the Steelers.

What exactly does it mean to be graded as an offensive lineman?

Many things are taken into consideration.

Agility. Awareness. Pass block speed. Pass block power. Run blocking. Movement in space. Pull trap ability. Strength. Technique. Size.

All these traits combine to make an offensive lineman a good or bad pass blocker and run blocker, which is what those ranking him are essentially looking for.

The cumulative score is the player's identity. It signals to coaches if the lineman can do his job well.

How do you score as a Christian?

For everyone who has been born of God overcomes the world. And this is the victory that has overcome the world—our faith. —1 John 5:4

TWO BITS, FOUR BITS, SIX BITS, A DOLLAR

If your friends or family watch you throughout the day, what ranking would they give you as a believer? Do you perform well in the categories of: Prayer. Church attendance. Bible reading. Witnessing. Compassion. Love. Integrity. Service. And the list can go on and on. Do people watch you? Of course, they do. You have an impact as an ambassador for the kingdom, so make it a positive one.

THE GATOR CHOMP

What do you expect from a true believer? Put your answers on your checklist and see if you can check them off. Live your life as if someone is always watching, even in the privacy of your own home. No one likes to get a bad score. You can never be perfect in your walk with the Lord, but you should try to be. Here are some tips to hold yourself to a higher standard.

1. Service: Be available at all times to your family and church. Your needs and wants should take a back seat to those who depend on you. When your pastor asks for volunteers to help at a church activity, consider raising your hand to volunteer. If you notice the leaves in the yard of a widow are piled high, do her a favor and go rake them for her. "For what we proclaim is not ourselves, but Jesus Christ as Lord, with ourselves as your servants for Jesus' sake" (2 Corinthians 4:5).

2. Prayer: The more you talk to the Lord, the stronger your relationship with Him becomes. If your children spoke to you two or three times a week, you would be concerned. God feels that way when you forget about Him. Make it a point to pray to your heavenly Father several times throughout the day. He always stands ready to help you with your problems, big and small. "If you abide in me, and my words abide in you, ask whatever you wish, and it will be done for you" (John 15:7).

3. Integrity: Do the right thing. Live with honor inside and outside of the home, and don't look for opportunities to make poor choices. Be honest. "The righteous who walks in his integrity—blessed are his children after him!" (Proverbs 20:7).

4. Attendance: Pouncey's success would never have happened if he never showed up for games and practices. If he hadn't, he probably would have been cut from the team. You cannot receive God's blessings and inspiration if you do not attend His house on a regular basis. This is where you are fed and encouraged. It's important to be in God's presence in order to feel His Spirit. If you are unable to attend in person, most churches offer livestreams of their services that can make you feel like you're in the building, or you can catch the recording of it later.

5. Giving: Offer your time and money for the service of the kingdom. Volunteer with a charity and tithe your money and do it with joy in your heart. "Each one must give as he has decided in his heart, not reluctantly or under compulsion, for God loves a cheerful giver" (2 Corinthians 9:7).

Being a Christian doesn't make you better than anyone else. But you are a child of God, and there are expectations that come with that. Ask those close to you their opinion of you as a follower. Be ready for the feedback and make needed adjustments if your grade is below par. Do your best to live up to what is expected and go the extra distance to post a 99 percent grade. A lot of spectators are watching your performance on the field.

DAY 36
SET THE RECORD STRAIGHT

January 1, 2010: Florida 51, Cincinnati 24

And you will hear of wars and rumors of wars. See that you are not alarmed, for this must take place, but the end is not yet. For nation will rise against nation, and kingdom against kingdom, and there will be famines and earthquakes in various places. All these are but the beginning of the birth pains. —Matthew 24:6–8

The 2010 Allstate Sugar Bowl was never a contest from the beginning of the second quarter, and the Gators took a commanding 30-3 lead into the half.

Florida quarterback Tim Tebow and the Gator offense set several Sugar Bowl records, including running all over the Bearcat defense for 659 total yards. On a personal note, Tebow set a Sugar Bowl and Bowl Championship Series (BCS) record with 482 yards passing and 533 total yards. His 320 yards passing in the first half also established a record, as well as his twelve straight completions to begin the game.

When the game was over, the 65,000-plus fans at the Louisiana Superdome witnessed a record-setting performance from the Gators.

Boundaries are crucial in your success as a follower of Christ.

When you go out to war against your enemies, and see horses and chariots and an army larger than your own, you shall not be afraid of them, for the LORD your God is with you, who brought you up out of the land of Egypt. And when you draw near to the battle, the priest shall come forward and speak to the people and shall say to them, "Hear, O Israel, today you are drawing near for battle against your enemies: let not your heart faint. Do not fear or panic or be in dread of them, for the LORD your God is he who goes with you to fight for you against your enemies, to give you the victory." —Deuteronomy 20:1–4

TWO BITS, FOUR BITS, SIX BITS, A DOLLAR

Life in general has enough drama, but sometimes those we love the most raise our stress level. This can be family members, coworkers, or friends. Those with the best intentions can say or do things to hurt you. How do you protect yourself from emotional injuries without putting a strain on your relationships? God commands you to be humble and loving, yet He does not expect you to let people walk all over you like you are a doormat. When you pray and ask the Lord to help you establish healthy boundaries and set the record straight, this is the first step toward showing love to those individuals.

THE GATOR CHOMP

Boundaries. Some people like and respect them, while others may view your use of them as overly protective. But setting them the right way with healthy and spiritual boundaries gives you ownership of yourself and makes you responsible for when to say yes or no. Your choices have consequences. When you implement expectations for others or refuse to accept abuse or neglect, you are on the right path toward goodness and love. Are these necessary to be a happy Christian? Yes. Here are some tips on how to set boundaries and establish them for yourself.

1. Assess: When you realize that a relationship, whether formal, romantic, platonic, or professional, has taken a turn for the worse, go to God in prayer. Step back and recognize how it makes you feel. Has someone turned their back on you? Why did this happen? Do you want it to get better? Seek the Lord along with wise counsel from your pastor or a Christian counselor. Be smart and disclose only to people you know you can trust and who are for your success. Sharing your story with the wrong people will only add to your problems. If you don't know who to talk to, ask God to show you.

2. Define: This is where you take ownership of what belongs to you. Toss out of bounds anything you can't control. Your thoughts, feelings, and decisions are up to you. Don't let someone else tell you what to do or how to live your life. Your instructions for life are established in the Bible. There may be times you need to explain your boundaries to those in your life. If a friend pressures you to make a decision you know is wrong, then take a stand and do what is right. If you make sure they know your limits are clear, they will respect you for your convictions.

3. Hold accountable: This can be a delicate line to walk, but you must not back down. After careful prayer, be clear that others know what will happen if certain behavior continues. Christ preached to turn the other cheek, but He also stood up to those who did not see eye to eye with him. Walk away if you must. "Like a muddied spring or a polluted fountain is a righteous man who gives way before the wicked" (Proverbs 25:26).

4. Reward: On the other end, make the party involved aware that there are rewards if boundaries are honored. Keep in mind that this is not "Pavlov's dog" but a system to recognize honest attempts to change.

5. Examine: Are these boundaries working and effective? Are they too harsh or too lenient? Give it time to see if they are working or if adjustments need to be made. Never let them down, but you can open cracks as you notice improvements from those impacted.

Records are good but most will be broken. Some might stand the test of time. The same goes for boundaries. Set them accordingly with prayer and consideration. If they are broken, then consider the consequences. They are set for one purpose: your spiritual and mental health.

DAY 37
SINGIN' IN THE RAIN

September 21, 2002: Florida 30, Tennessee 13

Make a joyful noise to the LORD, all the earth! Serve the LORD with gladness! Come into his presence with singing! —Psalm 100:1–2

On this particular day, Rex Grossman gave one of the best performances of any Florida quarterback ever. The junior captain threw for 324 yards and completed 22 of 32 attempts with three touchdowns to lead the tenth-ranked Gators over No. 4 Tennessee 30-13 at Neyland Stadium in front of almost 103,000 fans.

What made this performance so outstanding? Grossman led the Gators to the win during a heavy downpour of rain. After a scoreless first quarter, the clouds opened up and the rain started to fall. The Gators felt at home in the rainy and swamp-like conditions.

In the second quarter, Florida put up 24 unanswered points, thanks in part to four Tennessee turnovers.

Fans referred to Grossman's ability to adapt to the circumstances and sling the ball all over the field in bad weather as "slingin' in the rain."

How well do you perform when life's storms roll in?

Oh come, let us sing to the LORD; let us make a joyful noise to the rock of our salvation! Let us come into his presence with thanksgiving; let us make a joyful noise to him with songs of praise! —Psalm 95:1–2

TWO BITS, FOUR BITS, SIX BITS, A DOLLAR

Storms. Lightning. Tornados. Earthquakes. Blizzards. Bad weather is unpredictable. Residents in the southern part of the United States are regularly exposed to heat and humidity. Those who live in the northeast are accustomed to snow and ice storms. And those who live in the northwestern part of America near the West Coast can experience all four seasons in one day. The same goes for life. When you think everything is going well, out of nowhere a tsunami of events can take a toll on your attitude. When the storms of life come your way, it can be hard to stay focused on your inner peace. But that is the key to weathering the storm.

THE GATOR CHOMP

When you have a song in your heart, you have spiritual shelter and solid ground to stand on, no matter how hard it rains. This does not mean your troubles float away, but it does mean you stay focused on what is important, and it can lift your spirits and keep you going.

1. Singing glorifies the Lord: When you lift your voice in song to Christ, you are bringing glory to His name. When you sing praise unto the Master, you are magnifying the King of Kings. Maybe you perform at church or only when you are alone in your car. There is no

wrong time or place to sing praise to Him. "Praise the LORD! For it is good to sing praises to our God; for it is pleasant, and a song of praise is fitting" (Psalm 147:1).

2. Singing encourages yourself and others: When you are feeling down, there is nothing more uplifting to yourself and those around you than to whistle a snappy tune that honors the Lord. It can be a fun song, one that makes you snap your fingers, clap, or raise your hands. You can encourage others and be a fantastic witness to unbelievers. "But I will sing of your strength; I will sing aloud of your steadfast love in the morning. For you have been to me a fortress and a refuge in the day of my distress" (Psalm 59:16).

3. Singing gives you joy: Scripture tells us that singing leads to joy—and joy leads to singing. It's a wonderful circle of praise. If you are struggling with being happy, sing. If you are happy, sing. It can be contagious to those around you. "I will sing to the LORD as long as I live; I will sing praise to my God while I have being" (Psalm 104:33).

4. Singing strengthens your soul: All college football players are strong. Athletes must work out and eat right so they can be prepared to play the game. Take the necessary steps to keep your faith strong. One of the best ways to do this is to keep a song in your heart. When you combine singing praises with your daily Bible reading, prayer, and church attendance, you will find yourself gaining strength to face life's rainy conditions. "I will sing to the LORD, because he has dealt bountifully with me" (Psalm 13:6).

5. Singing pours rain on the devil: The enemy hates it when you show love and adoration to the King of Kings. The devil will never put a glorious song in your heart. He will try to flood your mind with music that does not lift up the name of God. Be careful what your ears are subject to on the radio and in your home. "Oh come, let us sing to the LORD; let us make a joyful noise to the rock of our salvation!" (Psalm 95:1).

You don't have to be a Dove Award–winning vocalist to sing praises unto God. He doesn't care about the quality of your voice. He just wants to hear it from you. Music is one of the best ways to lift you out of your loneliness and discouragement. Grossman played one of the best games ever in the middle of a downpour. You too can overcome the storms and sing in the rain.

DAY 38
IT'S ALL IN GOD'S TIMING

October 30, 1993: Florida 33, Georgia 26

For the vision is yet for an appointed time; But at the end it will speak, and it will not lie. Though it tarries, wait for it; Because it will surely come, It will not tarry. —Habakkuk 2:3 NKJV

This rivalry game was played in a muddy downpour at the Gator Bowl in Jacksonville, Florida, in front of more than 80,000 fans. Head Coach Steve Spurrier had to pivot from his prolific passing style of offense to a ground control running game in the slop.

He called on running back Errict Rhett, who turned in a performance to remember. The 5'11", 210-pounder from Hollywood, Florida, carried the ball an amazing 41 times and churned out 183 yards with two touchdowns as the Gators dominated the time of possession with almost 35 minutes.

In the third quarter, the Gators put together a drive for the ages. Rhett toted the pigskin 13 times and gained 41 yards in a 21-play, 80-yard drive that ate up 11 minutes of the clock. The drive culminated when Rhett plowed into the end zone from a yard out to increase the Gators to a 10-point lead over Georgia.

Bulldogs quarterback Eric Zeier led his team into Florida territory trailing 33-26 with less than a minute to play. He connected with receiver Jerry Jerman in the end zone for what was thought to be a potential game-tying touchdown with five ticks left to play in regulation.

But Florida cornerback Anthone Lott had called a time out right before the ball was snapped.

On the next play, Lott was flagged for a pass interference call and gave the Bulldogs one more shot at the end zone. Zeier's pass was incomplete, and Florida held on to win the game.

Had Lott not signaled for a time-out, Georgia would have had a chance to tie the game with an extra point kick. But quick thinking to stop the clock saved the game for Florida.

To everything there is a season, A time for every purpose under heaven. —Ecclesiastes 3:1 NKJV

Has God ever come through for you at just the right time?

TWO BITS, FOUR BITS, SIX BITS, A DOLLAR

Sometimes it's tough to trust God when you know you are running out of time and things look hopeless. You hope and pray the Lord will show up before it's too late. If He could just give you a sign to let you know your situation is under control, you feel like you could get some peace. But God's plan is often different, better, and more creative than anything you could ever dream up on your own. Will you signal for a time-out, or will you wait on Christ and His timing?

THE GATOR CHOMP

Is God trying to teach you a lesson? Perhaps He wants you to show total dependence on His will and not yours. No one likes to wait, but life happens in His timing. He will show up and call the time-out at the exact right moment. At the perfect moment. Don't make tough decisions without prayer, and never make one in the spur of the moment. Take into account these suggestions when you wait on God's timing.

1. Don't worry: Do not fret about the future. This doesn't mean you don't make any plans, but be sure to invite God to the planning meeting. Ask Him to lead you to the right college, the right career, and the right person handpicked just for you. Remember God is in control, and He will lead you if you trust Him to. Never force something to happen that He has not ordained in your life.

2. Praise while you wait: When life gets tough and you don't know what to do, praise God anyway. Praise Him before you know what He's going to do in your life. Give Him honor and glory in all you do, and He will make sure you make the right play at the right time. Trust Him and ask Him to help you obey and walk through the doors He opens for you.

3. Exercise patience: Good things come to those who wait. But our current society promotes a fast-paced lifestyle, and this makes us less patient. It's OK to have desires and want things to happen right away, but remember that your life is in God's hands. If you don't land that perfect job, consider that God has bigger plans for you. Wait on His timing. "Wait on the LORD; Be of good courage, And He shall strengthen your heart; Wait, I say, on the LORD!" (Psalm 27:14 NKJV).

4. Strengthen your character: While you wait on God's plan to develop, take every opportunity to read and study His Word and go deeper in prayer. Don't get ahead of His plan or get in the way. Trust Him to call the right play. Your plan may be completely different from what He has in mind.

5. Follow His lead: He is the Good Shepherd and will not lead you astray. Pray about your future goals and ask Jesus to make the way straight. "Trust in the LORD with all your heart, And lean not on your own understanding; In all your ways acknowledge Him, And He shall direct your paths" (Proverbs 3:5–6 NKJV).

Lott called time-out at the perfect moment in the game. If he had not followed his instinct and recognized the defense was not prepared for the play, Florida might have lost the game. You must do the same. Know the signs and follow the leading of the Holy Spirit. Wait on God to call your time-out. He always knows what will happen next.

DAY 39
WHAT WILL BE YOUR LEGACY?

November 22, 2008: Florida 70, The Citadel 19

One generation shall commend your works to another, and shall declare your mighty acts. —Psalm 145:4

Every Florida Gator fan knows who George Edmondson was. He may have been an insurance salesman from Tampa, Florida. But to Gator Nation, he was a legend.

Known as "Mr. Two Bits," he was considered to be the unofficial cheerleader for Florida from 1949–2008. Edmondson attended military school at The Citadel until the start of World War II when he enlisted in the United States Navy and became a pilot in the Pacific theater.

He came home from the war and began working in insurance. But his life got a little more interesting after a friend gave him a ticket to see the Gators host The Citadel in the season opener in 1949.

Florida fans had low expectations for the season since the Gators had posted a losing record the year before. They even booed the team and coaching staff before the game started.

Edmondson took it upon himself to stand up and cheer, "Two Bits! Four Bits! Six Bits! A Dollar! All for the Gators, stand up and holler!"

The Gators won the game, and the crowd appreciated his enthusiasm so much he returned the next week. He continued to lead the cheer and bought season tickets for the 1950 season.

Edmondson became popular and started to walk around the stands to lead the cheer in different sections of the stadium. He always waited for a break in the action on the field and got the attention of fans with an orange-and-blue sign that read "2 Bits" and blew a whistle.

Then the cheer broke out, and the fans followed his lead. He waved his arms, pumped his fists, and yelled as loud as he could.

Over the next several decades, his cheer became a tradition, and he even went on the road to some selected games and bowl appearances.

The university took notice and started to invite him to lead the crowd in pregame festivities in the 1970s. He would be introduced and run to midfield wearing a long-sleeved yellow dress shirt with an orange-and-blue tie combined with white-and-blue seersucker pants and black-and-white saddle shoes.

Edmondson blew his whistle and waved his arms to lead the entire crowd in the cheer. The tradition always happened right before kickoff, and it fired up the Gators.

The legacy was growing.

Through all the tradition and sportsmanship, Mr. Two Bits never wanted a dime for what he did for the morale of the team and fans. He even insisted on paying for his season tickets like every other fan.

He was even offered a gig from the NFL's Tampa Bay Buccaneers that paid well, but he turned it down because he was a true Gator fan, and his enthusiasm could not be bought.

Mr. Two Bits announced his retirement at the end of the 1998 season. Head Coach Steve Spurrier presented him with the game ball during a ceremony on the field.

But he would still show up from time to time to lead the cheer from the stands.

At the end of the 2008 season, he retired for good.

The university showed its appreciation with a pregame ceremony before the last home game of the season against . . . none other than The Citadel.

The tradition had started sixty years before during a game against the same school he had attended before the war.

Although he was never a Florida student, he was named an honorary alumnus in 2005 and was inducted into the UF Athletic Hall of Fame as an honorary letterman in 1992.

He died in 2019 at age 97, and his death earned national television mentions.

Not every Florida fan knew his name, but they remembered him for what he did at all home games. What will you be remembered for?

And what you have heard from me in the presence of many witnesses entrust to faithful men, who will be able to teach others also. —2 Timothy 2:2

TWO BITS, FOUR BITS, SIX BITS, A DOLLAR

Maybe you are doing well in school or your job. The ball is on your side of the field. You don't have the luxury of massive blockers to clear the way for you to make it to the end zone. The entire game is up to you. Make it count.

THE GATOR CHOMP

You are solely responsible for your reputation; it's on you to give the best effort. Only you can control your attitude and outlook. Here are some ways to get the attention of the crowd and wave your arms with enthusiasm to encourage everyone to cheer for the Lord.

1. Inspire others: The world sees enough negativity. Make the effort to be positive and show joy and compassion in your walk every day. Be a consistent inspiration every day. If people always wonder what mood you're going to be in tomorrow, you need to make a change today. Be someone others can always count on to be a light for Christ.

2. Forgive others: In the book of Ephesians, you are advised to pardon those who have wronged you. This can be difficult, but it is definitely worth the effort. Forgiveness takes away burdens and gives peace. Grudges are heavy. Toss them into the stands and rejoice because God showed mercy to you. "For if you forgive others their trespasses, your heavenly Father will also forgive you" (Matthew 6:14).

3. Love unconditionally: Show genuine affection and appreciation to your family. They won't be around forever. Love and care for those close to you, even if some have strayed from serving God. Be happy to see your loved ones and show them love and mercy no matter what they have done. They're family, and you may be the only Bible they ever read.

4. Give your time and money: God does not need your money, but you need His blessings. Maybe you think you can't afford to tithe, but as my pastor often says, you really can't afford not to. God will supply your needs when you put your trust in Him, and "He is able to do exceeding abundantly above all that we ask or think" (Ephesians 3:20 KJV). Find a way to give back to the kingdom of God, and use your talents for Him.

5. Show the way: If you're a young adult, be a leader to your friends. Invite them to church and show them the love of Christ. If you're a husband and father, God has entrusted you to be the model for your family. Teach them to always put God first and to show kindness to others. Be someone they can come to for comfort and advice. Pray with them and read the Word together. Play by the rules God has given you in His Word. Be honest. Be dedicated. Show respect and humility. Pray and be faithful to attend church. The journey's reward will be worth it all.

Mr. Two Bits never aspired to become a cheerleading legend, but one ticket from a friend changed his life. He followed his passion, and he was loved and respected by Gator Nation for many years. When you take your flight to heaven, how will you be remembered? Make it your goal to leave a legacy that points others to Christ. "Well done, thou good and faithful servant . . . enter thou into the joy of thy lord" (Matthew 25:21 KJV).

DAY 40
LOCK ARMS AND STICK TOGETHER

Every Game at The Swamp

Above all, keep loving one another earnestly, since love covers a multitude of sins. Show hospitality to one another without grumbling. As each has received a gift, use it to serve one another, as good stewards of God's varied grace. —1 Peter 4:8–10

At the end of the third quarter of every Florida home game at The Swamp, something special always happens.

The Pride of the Sunshine, the University of Florida's marching band, plays the waltz-style song "We Are the Boys from Old Florida."

According to archives, the song was written by two UF students, Robert Swanson and John Icenhour, around 1919. The duo penned the words and tune originally for their barbershop quartet.

Others give credit for the Florida version of the tune to Thornton W. Allen, a composer of marching band music in the early twentieth century.

Basically, no one knows the true history of the song. But one thing is for sure. The University of Florida owns the rights to its band arrangement while the words are in the public domain.

None of that really matters when the student body rises to lock arms and sway back and forth as they sing the song together.

It has been a tradition since the 1930s.

No matter the score. No matter the conditions. No matter the circumstances.

In the 1970s, the tradition of playing it at the end of the third quarter started. Before that, it was played at random, and no one could prepare to be present or to lock arms.

Imagine 88,000 screaming fans decked out in orange and blue. The third quarter comes to a close on a bright sun-filled Florida Saturday afternoon.

Then you hear the song start as they begin to sway, joining arms with friends and even some folks they may not know.

We are the boys from old Florida,
F-L-O-R-I-D-A.
Where the girls are the fairest,
The boys are the squarest
Of any old state down our way.
We are all strong for old Florida
Down where the old Gators play.
In all kinds of weather . . .
We'll all stick together . . .
For F-L-O-R-I-D-A

Take note that the word *together* is held out for a few seconds while everyone holds their lean as a symbol of strength in numbers.

Does this describe you? Do you stand with your brothers and sisters, no matter the circumstance? No matter the score?

This is my commandment, that you love one another as I have loved you. Greater love has no one than this, that someone lay down his life for his friends. You are my friends if you do what I command you. —John 15:12–14

TWO BITS, FOUR BITS, SIX BITS, A DOLLAR

A true friend is a rare treasure. Walter Winchell once said, "A real friend is one who walks in when the rest of the world walks out." Life will throw situations at you and your friends that are unpredictable. But real friends stick together through the good times and the bad. They tell each other when they mess up, and they listen when times get hard. They also pray for each other and lift each other up.

THE GATOR CHOMP

Can your friends depend on you to always be there for them? When life gets tough for those you love, do you tuck and run, or do you take the time to offer a kind word and a shoulder to lean on? Do you pray with them and offer a helping hand? Being a true friend takes character, patience, understanding, and selflessness.

1. Establish boundaries: Be a friend but draw the line when they try to steer you in the wrong direction. For example, never agree to take part in something that is illegal or immoral. Be wise and follow God's Word when your friends do wrong. True friends will never put you in a compromising situation.

2. Show forgiveness: C. S. Lewis once profoundly said forgiveness is "a beautiful idea until we have to practice

it." Forgiveness takes humility, and if you want to be a true friend, you will need to practice it faithfully. God has called you to show mercy just as He did. "Be kind to one another, tenderhearted, forgiving one another, as God in Christ forgave you" (Ephesians 4:32).

3. Be an encouragement: It's easy to be a friend when times are good. But in those dark instances where defeat looms large, that is when friendship is put to the fire. Be there to help. This doesn't mean you justify a wrongful act, but it means you are there to provide support. Who knows? You might be in the same predicament one day. "A friend loves at all times, and a brother is born for adversity" (Proverbs 17:17).

4. Show respect: We often see sitcoms on television that portray a friend as someone who gets laughs by putting his friends down. This might be funny on TV, but it's not in real life. When you demean a person's value and worth, it can have long-lasting effects. If Christ died for you, then He also paid the same price for your friend. Show respect to your friends and let them know they are valued.

5. Be accountable: This goes both ways. If you see a friend who is about to make a mistake, it is up to you to warn him in love. He still has to make his own choices, and you can't control that. But you can show him love and offer to help him through a bad situation. True friends don't try to control each other, but they always have each other's backs. But you need to keep your friend's feet to the fire as much as possible. And on the other end,

be open to listening to a friend who does the same for you. "Iron sharpens iron, and one man sharpens another" (Proverbs 27:17).

Florida fans can always depend on the band to play "We Are the Boys from Old Florida" at the end of every third quarter. When the song ends, fans always stay ready in The Swamp to support their Gators throughout the fourth quarter. They hope for a win, but you can depend on them to be back the next week no matter the outcome. "In all kinds of weather . . . we'll all stick together."

Made in the USA
Monee, IL
07 July 2026

56551633R00115